Charles William Doubleday

Reminiscences of the Filibuster War in Nicaragua

Charles William Doubleday

Reminiscences of the Filibuster War in Nicaragua

ISBN/EAN: 9783337061760

Printed in Europe, USA, Canada, Australia, Japan

Cover: Foto ©ninafisch / pixelio.de

More available books at **www.hansebooks.com**

REMINISCENCES

OF

THE "FILIBUSTER" WAR

IN

NICARAGUA

BY

C. W. DOUBLEDAY

NEW YORK AND LONDON
G. P. PUTNAM'S SONS
The Knickerbocker Press
1886

PREFACE.

IN this narration of events that, in their day, attracted a large share of the attention of the civilized world, some criticism of the acts of a very remarkable man is necessarily included. Entertaining, as I did, a warm personal attachment for General Walker, whose character was singularly free from the petty traits and vices of ordinary men, and a high admiration for his splendid courage, I was, nevertheless, opposed to the course he adopted in the affairs of Central America.

My own somewhat Quixotic espousal of the "people's cause," as it was called, was prompted by youthful enthusiasm for that most fallacious of human illusions, popular liberty, and antedated Walker's appearance in the field by more than a year. During that time suffering and privation had only intensified my desire to see the people freed from the tyranny of a dominant ecclesiasticism.

When Colonel Walker's plans—confidentially unfolded to me, as hereafter related—were understood to include the ideas of conquest and absolute empire, I begged leave to withdraw from the enterprise. He persuaded me, however, to accept instead, an indefinite leave of absence. My return to him in his days of disaster only proves that my sympathies were stronger than my ethical sensibilities.

Should my plain criticism in any way offend those survivors of that heroic episode who entertain unqualified admiration for their chief, they will, I trust, after this explanation, credit me at least with honesty of purpose.

As for the opprobrious and unjust appellation "Filibuster," which attaches to Walker's name and to that of his adherents, and which, while denying its appropriateness, I have adopted in these memoirs, I have explained its origin and cause further on.

Whatever stigma unjustly attaches to it was shared by valued comrades, whose bones will not on that account rest less peacefully beneath the soil of their adoption. I would not, by seeking to deny the consequences, seem to avoid complicity in their acts, but would rather emphasize, by the adoption of the term, my

Preface. v

preference for an association with the memories of heroes.

The survivors of those who exhibited such courage and fortitude in the " Filibuster " expeditions to Nicaragua, may feel that in connection with a narration of events the names of many who so heroically participated should be mentioned. A just attention to such a claim would, however, convert these personal reminiscences into an historical record, and enlarge the book beyond the limits designed. The attention of the American reader is respectfully called by the author to the substance of his remarks in the appendix ; relative to the desirability of an American inter-oceanic canal across Nicaragua, as a measure equally demanded by the exigencies of commerce, and of the national safety and honor.

C. W. DOUBLEDAY.

CLEVELAND, O., June, 1886.

CONTENTS.

CHAPTER I.

Voyage and arrival in the tropics—A revolution—La Democracia—Lively scenes and picturesque adjuncts—Novel method of landing 1

CHAPTER II.

Bathing under difficulties—Lake Nicaragua—Gorgeous scenic effect—A beautiful sunrise—Loss of baggage—Philosophical reflections—Animated forest life—Adventure with monkeys—Recruiting for adverse factions in the same town 9

CHAPTER III.

Departure from San Juan—Rum and glory—Flattering reception at Rivas—March to Granada—War's desolation—A shot from the enemy—Reception at Granada—Contract for military service—*Captain de Rifleros* 24

CHAPTER IV.

Sharp-shooting—Death of Doctor Peck—Colonel Don Mariano Mendez—A Foray and its consequences—Killing of prisoners—Burning a hacienda—A perilous situation . . . 43

CHAPTER V.

Visit of the American Minister—Truce declared, for the occasion only—Major Dorse's insidious treachery—An affair in the suburbs—Death of Dorse—Cholera and other sickness—Radicate's fiasco—I form a native company of riflemen—Assigned to the "post of honor" 61

CHAPTER VI.

Evacuation of the cantonment at Granada—Severe fighting and loss in my company—A Bongo cruise on Lake Managua—An earthquake—Arrival at Leon—Amusements and gayety 78

CHAPTER VII.

El Tamarinda—Trip to Honduras—Return to Leon—Arrival of General Muños—Vacillating policy—Advent of the "Filibusters"—Their impressions of the country—Jarring councils—Military expedition to the Department Meridional—Night march—Capture of enemy's picket . . 94

CHAPTER VIII.

Battle of Rivas—Retreat to San Juan 117

CHAPTER IX.

Seizure of a Costa Rican brig—Burning of the barracks—Escape from San Juan—Death of Dewey—Dangerous navigation—In a fishing-smack—On the sick list—Preparations for another expedition 138

CHAPTER X.

Departure of the second expedition—Narrow escape of Colonel Ramirez—Land at San Juan—March out to meet the enemy—Battle of Virgin Bay—Visions of empire—I obtain a furlough 155

CHAPTER XI.

Quiet of home life—Review of the acts of Colonel Walker—His successes and subsequent reverses—My return to Central America—British interference—Operations on the River San Juan—Blown up—Return to the United States . . 170

CHAPTER XII.

The Americans beleaguered in Rivas—Accept terms from the enemy—They leave Nicaragua—Subsequent efforts at return—Tried for violation of the neutrality laws—Acquitted—An expedition from Mobile—Evading the revenue cutter—"Over the blue waters"—A shipwreck—Rescued—Life on a coral island—Return to Mobile—Take leave of Walker—His subsequent expedition and death . . . 192

Appendix 219

CHAPTER I.

Voyage and arrival in the tropics—A revolution—La Democracia—
Lively scenes and picturesque adjuncts—Novel method of landing.

" What is a man,
If his chief good and market of his time
Be but to sleep and feed ?"

IN the early spring of the year 1854 I had taken a trip from the mining camps on the Tuolumnè River down to San Francisco.

I had been among the earliest invaders of those sylvan solitudes, which the *aura sacra fames* had converted from the peaceful abode of the acorn- and root-eating Digger Indian to that of the pork- and hard-tack-subsisting miner, the pioneer band, usually composed of the nomadic pike, or still more gypsy-like *Gambusino* from the Mexican State of Sonora.

To have a glimpse of the unaccustomed life of the city was the only reason for leaving my beloved haunts "'neath the greenwood tree," and, as the hurry and activity of city life was sure to pall upon me in a very short time,

I took care to see all that might interest me as quickly as possible. With this end in view, the morning after my arrival I had wandered towards the quays, and soon became interested in watching the busy throng of passengers embarking on the Pacific mail steamer, the smoke from whose funnels proclaimed her near departure for her distant port over the wide sea. She was bound for San Juan del Sur, a port in Nicaragua,—a land of the tropics,—a land, moreover, where the dulcet language of the Spaniards, with which I was familiar, was spoken, and where the genius of the *dolce far niente* presided. Why should not I, who had no ties to keep me in any particular place, subject only to the whim of the moment, go aboard, sail away, and wander among the tropical forests, as I had already done over those vast regions, inhabited by wild game and wilder Indians, that lie between the Mississippi River and the Pacific Ocean? Or, should Nicaragua prove uncongenial, I could continue my way to the United States, and look upon the faces of loved parents, ere again returning to my life of mountaineering and hunting. The thought was quickly father to the deed, and within an hour I was on board with my worldly effects. Very soon we were careering over the majestic bosom of the Pacific Ocean.

Voyages have been described *ad nauseam*. This was by no means my first, and the usual accompaniments of sea-sickness, flying fish, porpoises, *et id hoc*, failed to interest me as much as did the sound of the anchor chains running through the hawse-holes, proclaiming our arrival and anchorage in the Bay of San Juan.

The stoppage of the ceaseless jar of engines and of the forging motion of the vessel was very welcome, and enhanced the pleasure imparted by the sounds wafted from the shore through the tranquil air of the early morning.

First the awakening gun, and then the notes of the reveillé, substantiated the expectations, excited by the captain of the steamer, concerning the condition in which we should probably find the Transit Company's affairs. When he had left this post a month previously, since which time there had been no opportunity to receive news of the progress of events, the Democratic, or people's, party in the State had resorted to arms in order to seat the president-elect. The president in office, whose term had expired, supported by the Church, whose policy he sustained, had refused to abdicate the office.

Either the exigencies of war or its violence might readily have necessitated the horses and wagons, by aid of which we were to obtain transport over the twelve miles of road between San Juan and Virgin Bay, the point of departure for San Juan del Norte, or Greytown, on the Atlantic seaboard. For my part, so much had the captain interested me by his account of the haughty and tyrannic action of the party in power, backed by the dominating hierarchy, who sought to restrain the liberal measures advocated by the people's champions, and of the determination of the latter to achieve their liberties or suffer death, that I was already strongly inclined to join the Democrats in their struggle.

The arrival of the company's agent on board the steamer soon put us in possession of all the news. The Democrats had in successive days' fighting forced their enemy back into the city of Granada, to the very borders of the lake, but their losses and the severe wounding of their gallant leader had so crippled them, that any attempt to force a final issue at this time would have been imprudent. They had therefore gone into cantonments in the upper end of Granada, known as Jalteva. Each party was now busy in fortifying its respective position. President Chamorro, the head of the Church party, in order to strengthen his hardly pressed army, had withdrawn the garrison which the government usually kept at San Juan, and the Democrats, who assumed the responsibility of public affairs from their seat of government at Leon, had promptly occupied the place, and were prepared to protect, at all hazards, the treasure of the Express Company and the property of the Transit Company.

While the agent was on the deck of the steamer, giving us this hasty account of the condition of things ashore, the brilliant tropical sun shone above the dense foliage that nearly encircled the little town and bay, and illuminated with unusual splendor—at least to our eyes—the luxuriance of the vegetation, and the animated scene on the sunny beach a few yards distant.

The semi-monthly arrival and departure of the steamer was for the inhabitants the event to which all intermediate days led up, the intervals between these important crises being mostly passed by them in sleep. Just now, however, owing to the presence of the newly-arrived garrison of Democrats, flushed with victory and newly acquired power, the place was unusually wide-awake. As there was no wharf in this remote though long-established port, a primitive method of landing the passengers was resorted to. They were conveyed in small boats from the side of the steamer, as near to dry land as the shelving sands and the high surf would permit, and were thence carried ashore upon the brown shoulders of the native boatmen. During the transit funny mishaps were not rare. These may be laid to the frolicsome spirit of these darkies, who, often finding themselves too heavily weighted, or, again, feigning to be choked by the too tightly clasping arms of some timid female, would lose their balance, when porter and burden would go floundering into the limpid water. This performance always excited great merriment among the lookers on, and nothing worse happened to the luckless passenger than a wetting in the warm sea-water, and possibly a temporary loss of temper.

On shore, tents and booths were erected for the convenience of the venders of breakfasts and *aqua ardiente al fresco*. These were usually presided over by females whose limpid eyes and fascinating smiles, when serving (*por un concideracion*) the susceptible miner, aided greatly in the disposal of the more substantial viands, which were sought as a welcome change from the steamer diet.

For those disposed to more ceremonial and expensive habits, the hotels of the town offered a breakfast as elaborate in variety, if not in cookery, as could be desired.

At the table of one of these, with a high-sounding name, and furnishing, as its advertisement set forth, "all that the country afforded," I found, besides the usual hard-boiled eggs and harder chicken, a coterie of uniformed army officers, to whom, by the kindness of the purser of the steamer, I was introduced. When they found that I spoke their language and was, moreover, much interested in the popular cause for which they were contending, they became communicative about the cause and present status of the war, adding to the interest of what they told by that charming politeness which is characteristic of the educated Spanish-American.

The facility with which I had made up my mind to leave California may have been remarked; it will, therefore, cause no surprise when I record the fact that I at once decided to remain and join my fortunes to those of *La Democracia*, in the efforts to establish by the sword that will of the people which had been declared through the ballot.

Little time was left me for carrying my decision into effect, for the passengers, after a few hours' delay at San Juan, mounted horses and mules, and started on the journey of twelve miles over the transit road to Virgin Bay. The baggage had already been forwarded to that point. I wished to take leave of my fellow-countrymen and companions, albeit but of a few days, so I mounted the horse assigned me and accompanied them, intending when the baggage should be claimed at Virgin Bay, as we were informed it was to be, to withdraw mine and return thence to San Juan. I had been told that here might be picked up a scattered number of Europeans and Americans, who might be induced by the offer of good pay and adventure to join the Democratic army at Granada.

CHAPTER II.

Bathing under difficulties—Lake Nicaragua—Gorgeous scenic effect—A beautiful sunrise—Loss of baggage—Philosophical reflections—Animated forest life—Adventure with monkeys—Recruiting for adverse factions in the same town.

THE greater part of the journey to Virgin Bay was over the beautifully graded road made by the new Transit Company through the tropical forest. As I accompanied the rude and boisterous passengers—made more noisy by the liberal potations of *aguadiente* imbibed at San Juan, and their freedom from the restraint of life, a necessity within the narrow limits of the ship,—I consoled myself by observing the extreme beauty and tranquillity of the woods, with the lovely parasitical plants, climbing, trailing, swinging, on each side of the way, the bright sunlight darting between their leaves and casting shadows of arabesque pattern before and all about me.

I promised myself further pleasure in all this beauty when I should retrace my steps in solitude to San Juan. At Virgin Bay a renewal of the dissipation of San Juan was in order. I presented the remainder of my first-class cabin ticket to a friend of former days—Mr. Gibbs George, of Fulton, Missouri (I wonder if he is yet alive and remembers the occurrence), and was not sorry to see the boat leave the wharf, about midnight, freighted with my turbulent fellow-voyagers. The fatigue of a day of such diverse and arduous experiences soon dissipated the slight sensation of loneliness which accompanied me to the hard couch assigned me at the rather squalid hotel.

No amount of exhaustion, however, could long withstand the combined attack of the myriad of fleas with which the bed was infested, and, after a restless night, I arose with the first streak of dawn, and wended my way through the now silent and deserted street to the shore of the lake. My purpose was to seek relief from the soreness inflicted by my tormentors, by a bath in the limpid water. The pleasure and relief which I had hoped to derive from the bath were checked when, after my first plunge, I observed an attendance of large and repulsive-looking fish. Seeing a female of mahogany-colored complexion in the act of filling an earthern jar with water near by, I asked her what kind of fish they were. "They are sharks," she replied, "and they will eat you if you do not come out of the water."

I stood not on the order of my going, and learned afterwards that the sharks came up the San Juan River from the Atlantic Ocean into this large inland lake. The possibility of finding them in fresh water had not before occurred to me. As I was about to retrace my steps to the hotel, the peculiar brilliancy of the tropical sunrise arrested my attention. In the background, on what seemed to be the farther shore of Lake Nicaragua, a serrated ridge of extinct volcanic peaks stood up in the clear ether; the sunlight, streaming from behind and between them, irradiated the landscape without dazzling the eye of the beholder. The grandeur of these giant volcanoes, and their power of projection upon the vision, was startling. They caused comparatively distant objects to seem as near as those close at hand. Out of the centre of the tranquil lake, which occupied the foreground, the cone of the extinct volcano Ometepec rose straight up in the form of an obelisk, and with approximate symmetry. Its side and base down to the water were draped in the exuberant foliage of the tropics, while its tapering bare gray summit towered to the skies. No movement except the flicker produced by the sunlight on the slightly rippling surface of the lake disturbed the grand solemnity of the view. The general effect, in the clear atmosphere, of the grouping of such mountains I have nowhere seen equalled, except among the snow-capped ranges of Switzerland, and these, though not less grand than the Nicaraguan chains, are of a wholly different type, are surrounded by a different atmosphere, and clothed with a different vegetation. I turned from the lovely panorama with regret, once more to plunge into the business of life, with its turmoils and disappointments.

On presenting my baggage-check at the office of the company, I was informed that in consequence of the general inebriety of the passengers, many of whom were in no condition to see to their effects, it had been deemed best to forward all the baggage to the Atlantic steamer. No telegraph existed in those days, so I could not reclaim mine on this side of the company's offices in New York. This was a severe blow to me. I had a handful of loose coin in my pocket, but the few hundred dollars I possessed, with some valuable gold specimens, and a very good outfit of clothing, were in my trunk. No legal relief was to be had. As expostulation was unavailing, I turned on my heel and left the office. I have never heard what became of my effects. Drunkenness has never been among my sins, but I had to suffer for the faults of others, and trust to what Mr. Emerson would designate the law of compensation in human affairs for balancing the account.

After paying my bill at the hotel, and purchasing a quantity of fruit and cooked viands in the market, which I tied in my handkerchief, and seeing that my revolver was properly loaded, I threw over my shoulders the light *serape*, or blanket, of which my camping habits had taught me the value, and leisurely began to retrace my previous day's journey through the woods to San Juan. Having gone far enough to secure quiet and isolation, I seated myself in the shade of a gigantic seiba tree, near the bank of a rippling stream, and ate my breakfast amid the forest solitudes, undisturbed by the thought of my limited pecuniary resources. I had rather more than the traditional twenty-five cents with which self-made men have founded their fortunes when they crossed their Rubicon. Health and that confidence of youth which I had trusted before, in more forlorn situations, sufficed, with a philosophic disposition, to enable me to dismiss all care.

To the dreamer of pantheistic proclivities there is, indeed, a solace and affinity in nature, breathing of a presence dim and shadowy, connected by mysterious yet sympathetic chords with the human organism. Science vainly strives to analyze such feelings, and as vainly bids us ignore them. In such moments we seem to grasp a remote past of our being. Sensation and the trivial surroundings of daily life are for the time disregarded; the potentialities of existence seem to have expelled the myriad petty worries of ordinary life, and we find ourselves in the presence of that mysterious *Nirvana*—source of past and final rest.

In such musings, congenial to my habits of thought from earliest youth, though sadly out of joint with the practical spirit of the times, I passed many hours in this tranquil spot, until the slanting beams of the sun warned me that my journey was nearly all before me. As I had determined to sleep in the woods, in order to enter San Juan and pass the military outpost by day, instead of by night, I proceeded leisurely on my way. I encountered no human being, but in no wise lacked company, and of a very animated kind. My foot-falls made very little noise, and as the various native denizens of this vast tropical forest were seldom molested by the native people, I found the trees full of gayly-plumaged macaws, parrots, and various other birds whose names I did not know. Rolling in the gravel of the road, or digging among the roots by the wayside, I observed many of the kinds of animals which I had hitherto only seen through the bars of cages in travelling menageries or shows. Armadillos, ant-eaters, the guatuso, peccaries, or wild hogs, and many other kinds I passed, intent usually on seeking their evening meal; while the monkeys seemed to rise from the earth and fill the tree-tops every step of the way. These monkeys alone seemed to pay any attention to my passage over the road, chattering and using threatening gestures, ludicrous considering the panic of fear that followed any assumed aggressive action of mine.

As the sun, sinking behind the tree-tops,

warned me of the approach of night, I found myself crossing a little rustic bridge, thrown over a clear stream, on the farther bank of which I descried what on investigation proved to be the remains of a woodman's cabin. In the immediate vicinity of this the trees had been cleared away, probably, in part, for the construction of the bridge and hut, which latter, though deficient in roof or door, was not to be despised as a kind of fortress. The four walls opposed a barrier against any possible sudden inroads of wild beasts; besides that, the fire-place, and the four posts, over which a stretched bullock's hide still remained, might be counted as a fair preliminary preparation for fire, light, and a bed. I soon collected a quantity of dried wood, and improvised a barricade for the door-way. Then, as my labors and my walk of about eight miles had somewhat fatigued me, I determined before climbing over the wall, to bathe in the limpid pool near the bridge.

While engaged in putting the cabin in a condition for defence, I had noticed that my proceedings had been watched with apparent interest by an ever-increasing throng of monkeys. As I threw my clothing on the bank, taking the precaution, acquired by long habit rather than any apparent need at the present time, of placing my revolver in the hollow of a tree that overhung the pool, I saw that there was a growing disposition on the part of my simian neighbors to an aggressiveness that their numbers might make formidable. The divesture of the distinctive badge for which we are indebted to the tailor, increased their boldness, and I had been in the water only a few moments when a long-legged miscreant, volubly chattering with his comrades, advanced, seized part of my clothing, and lost no time in making off with it. This was indeed depriving me, like Sampson of old, of my chief source of strength, for, *in puris naturalibus*, I was evidently regarded as merely some stray Dryopithecus of a Miocene age, insignificant from the remoteness of my consanguinity. The situation had become rather critical. Taking steady aim at the thief as he paused at the first branch of the tree he was climbing, I fired, and had the satisfaction of seeing my shirt fall to the ground, while the wounded monkey, with alternate howls of fear and screams of pain and rage, vainly attempted to get out of my reach. Thanks to his broken shoulder, I quickly recovered my garment and, investing myself therein, my confidence was restored. Indeed, the cowardly gang had fled at the sound of the discharge, and the succeeding lamentations of their comrade, whose grotesque appeals and threats gave me a good deal of amusement as well as food for reflection. I believe it was my suspicion of a common humanity that induced me to offer him no further molestation, though I had not at that time read Darwin. In this tropical latitude night quickly succeeded day. The stars shone brilliantly above my roofless dwelling, but I sat long by the companionable fire reading by its light the fascinating pages of an odd volume of "Monte Christo," which I had retained among my meagre possessions.

After I had laid this aside and been sleeping some hours, I was awakened by a combination of howls and screechings which would have done honor to a tribe of wild Indians. Happily it was nothing more serious than the "baying" to the newly risen moon, or my flickering firelight, of the forest denizens. Loudest and most portentous of danger was the voice of the *Mono Colorado*, an exceedingly ferocious species of monkey, usually inhabiting mountainous districts. I arose and threw more wood on the fire, then, trusting to my walls and the monkey's fear of the blaze as obstacles to aggression, I soon again yielded to fatigue, and slept until the sunbeams penetrating between the logs of my hut awoke me. The remains of the stores I had provided on setting out furnished me with sufficient breakfast, and with renewed strength and hope I took up my way. An hour's walk brought me to the bridge crossing the little river a mile outside of San Juan. Here, on the journey to Virgin Bay we had seen the half-clad *lavaderas* of San Juan in picturesque groups, smoking their cigaritos and chaffing the returning passengers while resting from their labor of washing. Here also, where partial openings in the wood had admitted the sunlight, the flowering plants were most abundant and various. An apparently endless network of vines and interlacing branches of trees formed an arbor over the devious stream. Flower and leaf seemed to drape every thing but the silvery water rippling over its brown pebbly bed. Conspicuous amid the green foliage the deep blue flower of the indigo plant and the variously colored convolvulus had established themselves, the latter climbing along and over any thing that offered a support for its tendrils.

Amid this exuberance of tropic growth, the brilliant-plumaged and numberless macaws, parrots, parroquets, and an endless variety of other birds whose names were unknown to me, flitted to and fro, chattering in apparent enjoyment, and fearless of molestation in these their native haunts. I left the spot regretfully, and with it the seclusion I had enjoyed.

Now from a slight eminence I saw before me the town of San Juan, and the shimmering expanse of the blue ocean, along whose shores, far as the eye could reach, stretched the heavy green drapery of tropical foliage. A brief question or two by the guard sufficed as passport to the town, where I at once established myself at one of the principal hotels, and began canvassing among the foreign residents for recruits with which to form a company for the service of *El Ejercito Democratico.* I very soon found that I was not alone in this, to me, novel employment. A "Major Dorse," of Texas, and formerly, I believe, in the U. S. army, was eloquent in setting forth the advantages to be derived by a union of interests with the party which had the archives and official positions of the government in their possession, which had the powerful aid of the Church, and, what appealed still stronger to the sympathies of his German, Italian, and French hearers, the revenues at their disposal.

After the passengers had left Virgin Bay, the Democratic garrison of San Juan had been withdrawn, thus enabling us to present the unique spectacle of recruiting in the same town for each of the adverse factions. I found an able coadjutor in "Don Augustin," a gentleman of education and means, from Ohio, whose enthusiasm for the cause of the people made him willing to trust the Democratic government for the necessary outlay incurred in organizing a company for the service. Major Dorse was an able, though unscrupulous, soldier, skilled in the use of the rifle, and somewhat famous as an artillerist.

I could count myself his equal with the rifle, but lacked his gift of lying, for in him this faculty amounted to a gift, and was accompanied by all the good taste and judgment that could make it attractive to the undiscerning. He managed to enlist all of those whose nationalities my men designated as foreign, by which the intelligent reader will readily recognize that I had the Britons and Americans with me. Although Dorse's men were nearly double mine in point of numbers, I was waited upon by a delegation of jolly tars, who asked permission to begin the campaign by cleaning out what they termed "the bloody foreigners." I think it is M. Taine who remarks that a Briton always deems the place where he is as his home, and the other people foreigners. It took all my persuasive powers to make these uneducated men understand the difference between legalized warfare and vulgar throat-cutting. *Quien sabé?* as the Spaniard hath it.

Being fairly embarked in the narrative of this war of factions, I will, in the next chapter, endeavor to give some idea of the questions at issue, which by the leaders of the people were deemed of sufficient importance to justify the revolution inaugurated by them. I have no justification to offer, for my own part, in the war, for the days of chivalric sentiment are gone by, and even youthful ardor is not so extravagant as it used to be. "Peace has its victories as well as war," but I have sometimes thought, as I watched young men intent upon the tape recording the fluctuations of stocks, involving perhaps risks as great as those of the battle-field, that life for them, though not devoid of hazard and excitement, would never yield those supreme moments that lift men above petty personal cares.

CHAPTER III.

Departure from San Juan—Rum and glory—Flattering reception at Rivas—March to Granada—War's desolation—A shot from the enemy—Reception at Granada—Contract for military service—*Capitan de Rifleros.*

"To the wars, my boys, to the wars!
He keeps his honor in a box unseen
Who hugs his kicksey-wicksey here at home."

THE causes which led to a resort to arms for a settlement of the differences existing between the two political parties in Nicaragua in the year 1854, are the same as those inspiring nearly all the *prononciamentos* which so frequently disturb the tranquillity of the Spanish-American governments.

The descendants of the hidalgos, who in the "good old days" conquered the fertile provinces of the New World and governed them in the name of Mother Church and for the benefit of themselves and the Spanish crown, lost, in a great measure, their occupation when the colonies became independent, for under representative forms of government power had to be sought through the ballot, not through the favor of a single arbitrary sovereign. This often resulted in the elevation to office of men who, in courting popular favor and administering to the mass of the people, necessarily infringed on the self-established prerogatives of the aforesaid hidalgos and of the Church. The former, accustomed to consider the offices of the state as theirs by right, and the latter, always in alliance with those wielding the power and disbursing the revenues, viewed with disapproval the new order of things. Old-established customs were often abolished; laws were passed ameliorating the condition of the people—that is, freed them from burdens imposed in the interests of the seigniors and the hierarchy. These measures, always received with dislike by the classes referred to, were in this instance opposed in anticipation by President Chamorro, the magistrate in office, who, relying on the support of the clergy and his possession of the archives and various appurtenances of government, together with his command of the army, caused President-elect Don Francisco Castellón to be seized, and, with his most influential friends, to be conveyed to the Honduras frontier. The action was justified by a decree of banishment, procured with ease by the party in power, who, on the plea of military necessity, could manipulate the constitution to please themselves.

Castelloñ found ready sympathy in the Democratic president of Honduras, and could easily have obtained through him both men and money. Preferring, however, to rely on his own people and the justice of his cause, he boldly returned with his friends to his native city of Leon, where he received a complete ovation, and was at once installed by the authorities of the Occidental Department as President of the Republic. Knowing, from the attitude of the Church party, that one course only was open to him, he lost no time in organizing a volunteer army, at the head of which he placed the valiant General Don Maximo Jerez, the same who of late years, and until his death, represented Nicaragua at Washington.

Jerez met the enemy at Managua, the seat of government, and in a series of engagements pressed them back to Granada. Chamorro had provided for his final stand in that city by the transmission thither of the archives and military stores, by fortifying the plaza, and by collecting within the harbor the various craft which plied on the lake. By this last stroke he commanded the rich cattle estates of the Chontales district on the opposite shore, and could furnish his commissariat with supplies, otherwise difficult with an enemy in front of him. His situation, outside of these advantages, was well chosen. The barrier of the lake prevented the desertion of his troops, many of whom were forced levies, while the Democrats, in following him, were placing a greater distance between themselves and Leon, whence they derived most of their supplies of men and means. He was thus better prepared to contest the issue than if he had kept to the open country.

The Democrats, full of ardor and inspired by the justice of a cause which was manifestly a resistance of oppression, pressed after their enemies, whom, in consequence of their assumption of a kind of right divine to govern, they had nicknamed the " Legitimists," and would have sought a final issue in Granada by attempting to force the fortifications of the plaza ; but General Jerez, as wise as he was brave, foresaw the futility of such an attempt. His troops were in an exhausted condition, he himself temporarily incapacitated by a severe wound, and it was plain that the enemy had deliberately planned and strengthened themselves for such an emergency.

The Democrats, therefore, on their side, barricaded and loop-holed the self-same walls and houses that formed a barrier for their enemies, and in this close juxtaposition prepared for recuperation and further conflict.

It was at this crisis that I arrived and joined my fortunes, as already recorded, with the *Democracia*, or party of the people.

It was a relief to me, as I am sure it was to Major Dorse, when he was at last able to extricate his men from the influence of the rum shops of San Juan and the risk of collision with my party. The day after his departure we began our march for Granada, intending to go as far as the town of Rivas, distant about fifteen or twenty miles from San Juan, being the capital of this, the meridional department of the state, and garrisoned at the present time by the Democrats.

We had been directed to call upon the governor of the town, Don Justo Lugo, from whom we expected to receive the necessary arms and equipments with which to protect ourselves in traversing the debatable ground between that city and Granada.

Our first day's march was not quite in accordance with the military rules for the conduct of a march in an enemy's country. First, the men had, with singular unanimity, adopted the notion that a parting call at the whiskey shops was a necessary preliminary to a good start. Though their farewell potations doubtless gave an impetus to the forward movement, they caused a divergence from a straight line, which was not even partially corrected until we got beyond the last *pulperia* of the town. Don Augustin was very much scandalized at such behavior on the part of men embarked in a cause so sacred as that of ours. I managed, however, to excuse them to him, and promised better conduct as soon as we should have competent authority for restraining them.

To Don Augustin I had willingly accorded the nominal leadership of the party, acting myself as his lieutenant; the place was but a fair recognition of his ample disbursements of money for the cause. But I quickly perceived that whatever mantle of authority was in the future to be used in the subjection of these rude natures, would fall on my shoulders. It was not that my experience in commanding men was greater, but that I could adapt myself more readily to the emergencies sure to arise. Years of adventurous experience in the Rocky Mountains and early California placers had inured me to the exigencies of a life where eternal vigilance and promptitude of action could alone offer any guaranty of safety. I therefore, without effort or straining of authority, directed whenever it was necessary, leaving to Don Augustin the honor of leading the cavalcade whenever the spectacular effect was paramount.

That authority was most needed on this march will be obvious to the reader who has ever seen a party of sailors on horseback at the end of a spree.

By the time we reached the precincts of Rivas, on the morning of the second day's march, the men presented a more orderly appearance. We marched to the presidio with some degree of order, escorted by a gayly caparisoned troop of lancers who had been sent out to honor our entry. A throng of people had assembled in the plaza in front of the government residence, for the news of the accession of a body of "valiant American sharpshooters" to the cause of the people had not been permitted to go unheralded.

I was well contented to let Don Augustin be the hero of the occasion, for the truth is, I was a little ashamed of the appearance of our squad, though I had no doubt of their doing efficient service whenever occasion should require it. The occasion, however, was not without a certain solemnity and pathos, for this revolution was a supreme effort of an oppressed people to throw off the shackles of authority that had long restricted their just rights, and the interest and exultation they manifested at this espousal of their cause by strangers from over the sea, was not without its lesson to us.

The governor, accompanied by his staff, welcomed us in Spanish, and then said that his adjutant would more intelligently convey his thanks. At the same time he motioned to an individual at his side, whose remarkable appearance had called forth various comments from the Americans, who had already christened him "Napoleon," from a fancied resemblance of costume to that of the gray-eyed man of destiny. This individual, who, by the way, retained the nickname during years of service in connection with the Americans in Nicaragua, stepped to the front, his long sword and spurs jingling as he moved, and bowing with extreme courtliness, he delivered an address of welcome in very good English. The substance, however, was in true Spanish fashion, full of grandiloquent phrases, among which I remember that he assured us we were "worthy of acceptance as *victims* in the cause of Nicaraguan liberty"; and that our "heroic and martial appearance indicated that we were eager to sacrifice ourselves for the sacred cause," etc., etc. Don Augustin accepted the eulogy and welcome with a gracious reply. I felt that the affair was an excellent joke, especially the part of the speech referring to our martial appearance. The conclusion of the speeches was the signal for a hideous clang of all the church bells in the town and the simultaneous braying of two or three brass bands, after the fashion which we subsequently became pretty well accustomed to. I supposed that the demonstration was all right, and, though I could not quite understand it, began to believe that we had done something meritorious. The real meaning of this boisterous and exultant demonstration had, as I afterwards learned, a decidedly practical end. It was intended to inspire the weak-kneed with an idea of our strength, and to intimidate the disaffected.

Over and above all this, our reception was kind, and, after being furnished with such arms as the town could provide, with authority from the governor for using them, if necessary, in our own defence while traversing the country between Rivas and Granada, we set forth the next morning amidst the *vivas* of the populace.

For some distance we wound along the devious streets, bordered in places by gigantic columnar cacti of a century's growth, behind which stood the ancient and peaceful looking dwellings. It was difficult to realize while threading these tranquil precincts, that our mission was one of strife and bloodshed. When we emerged in the open country, quiet haciendas and herds of grazing cattle met our view. It was still in the early stage of the war, and the property near to Rivas remained undisturbed. At a subsequent period the track of war desolated these peaceful spots.

We encamped for the night at a pueblo, near the shore of Lake Nicaragua, and, as this was ground foraged by both factions, the landscape wore a different aspect. Blackened walls and devastated fields bore evidence to the destructiveness of war and partisan hatred. The inhabitants of the village had profited by their experience in one respect at least: they carefully avoided expressing either enthusiasm or enmity for us, not knowing what colored ribbons their next visitors might display. In their unprotected situation it was prudent to give neither party pretext for aggression. The next day's march gave further evidence, in the desolated country, of the ravages inflicted by civil war.

No sign of life appeared upon the dreary waste of what, judging from the remains of farm-houses and fallowed fields, had been the abode of industry and thrift. About noon the dull, ominous sound of cannon-firing was wafted over the dreary expanse to our ears, and we knew that we were approaching Granada.

In the middle of the afternoon the towers of the churches and the higher buildings became visible, and as we ascended some higher ground, Lake Nicaragua and its opposite shore lay before us; still nearer the red-tiled roofs and white walls of Granada reflected the rays of the declining sun.

After leaving Rivas, when it became necessary to use precautionary measures against a possible ambush, I had taken charge of the men, and had thrown out the necessary flankers to guard against surprise. One of these now rode to the head of the column, where I was leading the march, and reported the approach of a small troop of lancers with red pennons fluttering from the staffs of their lances. Although the color was that of *La Democracia*, which each of us wore around our hats and in the form of rosettes on our coats, the enemy's colors being white, I deemed it prudent to be ready to receive those who were approaching us either as friends or enemies. I therefore ordered the men to dismount and leave their tired horses under a small guard; then, taking an advantageous position, I awaited with loaded rifles the approach of the party. As soon as they came within half gunshot I stepped into the road and ordered them to halt. This they did, and the lieutenant in command rode up and touching his cap politely, informed me in Spanish that the general had been apprised by the governor of Rivas of our approach, and had sent him out to escort us into the cantonment. The guide whom Don Justo had furnished us at Rivas identified the lieutenant as belonging to our party, and we at once followed under the escort of his troop. As we approached the city more nearly, the peaceful aspect which it at first presented was changed by the appearance of the muzzles of a number of brass field-pieces protruding from improvised sand-bag batteries in the towers of two of the churches in the plaza, a plentiful sprinkling of heavier guns being discernible in different places in the city.

The lieutenant informed me that as the enemy had been reinforced the day before by a body of foreign riflemen and artillerists, the leader of whom had already exhibited his skill in the use of the battery, which he pointed out, in the church tower, we might expect to receive some attention from the same source while passing over a certain elevated plateau on the road in advance, at which point, he said, it would be well to increase our speed.

I, of course, assented, but did not think it necessary to translate the information for the benefit of the men and Don Augustin, who, now that the escort had assumed our guidance, had taken his place at the head of the column.

As we came to the highest place in the road

the lieutenant left me, and dashing to the head of his lancers they scurried over the ridge very quickly. I repeated in English the order he had given his men, to gallop, taking at the same time the rear of the column for myself. Most of the men were quickly over the brow of the hill and screened by intervening objects and the dip in the ground from further danger. But while some of the rear files were yet on the summit, I observed a puff of white smoke issue from the plaza, and a second or two afterward a round shot crashed through the tiles and adobes of the house beside which we were riding. It passed over our heads, struck the ground beyond, and ricochetted harmlessly away. Another followed, ploughing the road over which we had just passed, and then, we also were sheltered from further risk, having suffered no more damage than a plentiful sprinkling by fractured tiles and adobes.

This was an early initiation to our new profession, which the men seemed to accept as an excellent joke. I wondered why the lieutenant had not avoided, by a slight detour, a place on which the enemy kept their guns trained; but if the grinning natives of the escort expected to see any timidity, which would have been excusable among men most of whom had never before heard the whistle of a hostile shot, they must have been disappointed.

As we passed the outposts, I was gratified by the promptness displayed in turning out the guard, and the precise, soldierly observance of those forms and precautions deemed necessary for safety on such occasions by well-organized military bodies.

Our reception at head-quarters was imposing and kind, and we were dismissed to the quarters which had been assigned us, amid the ringing of bells and braying of brass instruments, intended to serve the purpose both of welcoming us and of striking "terror into the soul of Richard," on the other side the lines. Our men, however, evidently considered that we were the heroes of the occasion, and characteristically responded by hastening to get drunk.

Don Augustin and myself were active in equipping the men and instructing them in the effective use of their weapons. As there were only twenty of them—the nucleus of a larger force, we hoped,—drill, except in the simplest movements, was dispensed with.

The skill of Major Dorse as an artillerist was much vaunted, and I found that rumor had equally exaggerated my proficiency in the use of the rifle.

I felt that the paramount duty of Don Augustin and myself, at this time, was to obtain suitable terms and conditions of service for the men and ourselves. Otherwise we might find our efficiency for the peculiar service required of us impaired by our subjection to the orders of petty officers, whose commissions might outrank ours. I therefore urged Don Augustin, who spoke Spanish very well, to effect advantageous arrangements.

His reply was that "he came to serve for the honor and good of the cause," and that he was willing to accept the same terms as those granted to the native army.

As I was tired of working under an impracticable commander, I declined to accede to his views, and several of the more intelligent of the men told him bluntly that he was a fool, an exaggerated way of expressing their opinion that he was not fitted for his present position. I think he recognized his incapacity, and therefore begged me to do what I thought best, leaving him out of the organization.

I at once asked for an audience with General Jerez. He received me most kindly. He was confined to his couch by a severe wound, received in their occupation of the Jalteva. His head-quarters were in the Jalteva Church, and his audience-chamber was the large sacristy of the edifice. A suggestion of barbaric splendor was not lacking in this improvised camp of a soldier.

The sacristy being protected somewhat from the round shot of the enemy by the body of the church, which fronted the plaza, had been stored with fine pictures and the sacramental plate, and these gave an air of imposing richness and splendor to the apartment, in which were groups of richly uniformed general officers. On a couch, in an alcove, reclined the commanding officer. Those who remember General Jerez in the prime of his life will recall the intellectual splendor, if I may so express it, which beamed from his pale countenance, framed by ringlets of raven-black hair. He shook hands cordially, and courteously thanked me for the interest manifested by myself and friends in the people's cause. When I showed him the schedule I had prepared of the terms which I considered would be mutually advantageous for the proposed service, he quickly comprehended the detail. With his pencil, he added an increase of the pecuniary remuneration I had asked. He at once signed the document, and again expressing gratification at our advent, begged that I would always communicate directly with him concerning our requirements. I took my leave, much impressed with the refinement and courtesy of these people, whom Americans often thoughtlessly imagine to be as deficient in social graces as they are behind us in the march of practical civilization.

The contract provided for our exemption from any guard duty except over our own quarters, from all police or labor details, and exempted us from orders from any other than general officers. Hence questions of precedence and petty authority could not interfere with our seeking those " coigns of vantage " from which as sharp-shooters we might inflict most damage on the enemy.

The pay of the men was five times that of the native soldier. My own, that of my rank of full captain—*Capitan effectivo*, as it was expressed. My own name was also followed by the descriptive title " *El Capitan California*," and thus I was designated through the whole period of my service in Nicaragua by all the natives whether friendly or inimical.

I may as well state here that on my representing the service rendered by Don Augustin and his disinterested aims, he received reimbursement for his pecuniary outlay and the appointment as an aide on the general staff. In this position he did creditable service, until, becoming disillusioned of his ideal of liberty, he, some time afterwards, resigned, and, I believe, left the country.

CHAPTER IV.

Sharp-shooting—Death of Doctor Peck—Colonel Don Mariano Mendez—A Foray and its consequences—Killing of prisoners—Burning a hacienda—A perilous situation.

THE actual and relative situation of the contending parties at the time of my arrival in the Jalteva was not difficult to understand. Exhaustion occasioned by frequent encounters made rest and recuperation desirable. Neither party was in any thing like a fit condition to continue aggressive operations. The attention of both was therefore turned to the strengthening of their positions, the care of the wounded who filled the hospitals, and the recruiting of their depleted ranks.

Barricades were erected and walls loop-holed, and as the streets lying parallel with the lines of the contestants were raked by the grape and canister from the artillery, it became necessary to devise safer means of communication with the different parts of our cantonment. This was effected by piercing the thick adobe walls of the houses on one side of each of the main thoroughfares, making the opening large enough for soldiers to march through. Thus in a straight line from block to block we had a covered arcade, screened by the contiguous roofs and walls, and affording passage-way reasonably secure at least against small shot. A not infrequent occurrence was the passage through roof and wall of a twenty-four-pound round shot, scattering timbers and adobes in every direction, and of course dealing death and mutilation in its course.

The enemy had adopted the same method of shelter, but in crossing the streets transversely to our position the low breastworks, often breached by our cannon, afforded very imperfect shelter from our shot. Before the advent of Dorse's party in the plaza and ours in the Jalteva, the bungling aim of the natives commanding these defective places had not resulted in serious damage to those who unwittingly offered themselves as targets, but riflemen effected a serious change. The skipping and contortions which, as a rule, followed the sharp report of a rifle, was evidence of accuracy of aim, and though the sport was death to one party, repeating the fable of the boys and frogs, it seemed to afford great amusement to the other.

But this was a game at which Major Dorse and his men could play as well as we, and our accidents were probably quite equal to those of the enemy. So close were the barriers of each party to those of the other, that even the operation of thrusting a rifle through the loophole in a wall had to be performed quickly, or it would inevitably draw the shot of some lynx-eyed marksman of the opposite side, who had but to fire quickly at the loop-hole to insure his shot taking effect upon the person on the other side. In this way we suffered many casualties, my best marksman being struck below the eye by a rifle ball fired from the opposite wall.

I had one morning made the rounds as usual to the posts where the men were stationed, accompanied by Doctor Peck, a colored physician from Pittsburg, acting as a surgeon for the Democratic army. The doctor had asked leave to accompany me in order to see the different advanced posts of our army. As we were about to leave the barriers, an adjutant of Colonel Olivas, who was officer of the day, came up and informed me that the colonel desired him to say that a small party of the enemy had been detected near where we then were, cutting an opening through a wall on their side; behind this hole they had conveyed a gun of large calibre. Their intention was probably to obtain a range that would be destructive to some exposed point of our cantonment. The aide said the colonel wished me, if an opportunity should occur, to annoy them with some of my riflemen, until they could be checked later by a larger force.

We followed the aide, and quickly arrived where the blows of the picks and bars were easily audible in the wall on the opposite side of the street, and, as the wall on our side was loopholed for musketry, I had no sooner glanced through than I perceived, within a hundred feet of me, a squad of artillerists aligning a gun of twenty-four-pound-shot calibre, directly over our heads, probably at some point in our cantonment beyond us.

To me the most startling object in the group was the well-known figure of my quondam associate, Major Dorse, superintending the preparations for firing the piece. His long rifle rested across his left arm, and I experienced a spasm of regret as the conviction forced itself upon me that duty impelled me to shoot this dangerous foe of the party I had promised to aid. There was no evading my evident duty. I thrust my rifle through the loophole. The moments of life for this brave Texan did indeed seem to be few. Peck, who was watching from another loophole, as he saw me put the rifle through the wall, hastily begged me to let him make the shot. It was an easy one, and I was very glad to be spared the task which, necessary though it was, seemed like taking an unfair advantage. I relinquished the breech of the rifle, telling him, as I made way for him to take my place, to be sure and shoot the man who held the rifle. I cautioned him to be quick, for should they see the muzzle of the rifle projecting beyond the wall they would make short work of us. The doctor, however, did not understand "setting" the trigger, which, owing to the delicacy of the touch which releases the spring after this is done, is left until every thing else is adjusted. I quickly set it, but had scarcely relinquished the breech when I felt myself hurled with great force to the ground. Half stunned, my eyes and ears filled with the débris from the wall, I nevertheless knew what had happened. The fatal delay of Peck had given the enemy a sight of the rifle, and the gunner, slightly depressing his piece, had sent the shot from the place where the rifle projected at the wall. The ball had opened a large breach, and, as scrambling to my knees I peered through the dust, I saw Dorse, with rifle at his shoulder, watching for some moving object to aim at. Not wishing to be that object, I kept close under the unbreached portion of the wall, where Peck lay, slowly straightening in the rigidity of death. The ball had merely grazed his forehead, the concussion probably producing his death. The aide-de-camp and myself managed to drag his body away from the aperture, and, as a party of our troops had arrived, the fight soon became general.

Among the officers were men of education and refinement, usually soldiers of experience rather than of inclination; for, in the fierce partisan wars that so frequently devastate the Spanish-American republics, a man can often safeguard more certainly both property and person by joining the army than by staying at home. A neutral is usually considered legitimate prey by each party in the strife.

The ideal of the soldiers of *La Democracia* was Colonel Mariano Mendez, the pennon of whose lance had, during the last thirty years, fluttered to the breeze on nearly every battlefield of his native Mexico and of Central America. In the middle ages he would have been designated a soldier of fortune.

His love of strife, and—owing to his improvident habits—his generally destitute condition, impelled him to fight wherever and whenever he saw an opportunity. His great skill in the use of sword and lance, combined with a cunning and daring that often insured success in enterprises distasteful to more able but more scrupulous men, assured him a numerous following of adventurers. He was the son of a Spanish cavalier and an Indian mother, singularly handsome of form and face, though both were seamed with the scars of many battles. His complexion and raven locks, now streaked with gray, betokened Indian blood, while his exceedingly graceful horsemanship and skill in the use of weapons were probably an inheritance from noble Spanish ancestry. He was remorseless and cruel; his mode of warfare was savage rather than civilized; his name was a terror to the enemy;

and, although great license was permitted by the authorities on each side, General Jerez often found it difficult to restrain Mendez even within the generous limits.

This somewhat formidable personage had conceived a liking for me, possibly on account of my proficiency in the use of the rifle, a weapon he knew nothing about; I certainly admired the reckless and graceful soldier, whose atrocities were, so far, only matters of hearsay to me. He united with his warlike traits the gentler gifts of the troubadour and improvisatore, and frequently invited me to join the gay officers who were continually serenading those ladies who, during this period of inaction, shared the life of the camp with their husbands and fathers.

The mere life of the camp, despite the numerous daily casualties, which, taken in the aggregate, were more serious than would have been the disasters of a pitched battle, was monotonous to those who sought "the bubble reputation," or the excitement of a general engagement. However, the frequent sorties by detached forces, either for the purposes of forage and the commissariat, or to check an encroachment on our lines, or to harass a weak point of the enemy's, offered opportunities for winning local glory or getting knocked on the head; that was the business I had engaged for, and as the duties of the men required but little supervision, I often volunteered my services for these expeditions.

Mendez, who generally reserved himself for those occasions in which glory and profit could be combined, had casually asked me if I cared to join him in a project he had on hand, which would require a considerable force, and would detach us from the support of the main body of our army,—an affair, he said, in which the rifles could be of great service.

I readily agreed to go, and promised that as many of the rifles as chose to volunteer should accompany me. The result was that all volunteered. General Jerez granted leave, though he was doubtful whether Mendez and myself would agree about the management of the affair, the plan of which included the destruction of the buildings and the capture of the rich stores of cacao on the estate or hacienda of Don Fruto Chamorro, the president of the opposing faction.

The hacienda was situated beyond the farther extremity of the enemy's lines, and on the shore of the lake. Although it contained valuable stores, owing to its distance from our army and the proximity of the plaza, whence it could if necessary be reinforced, it had not been well guarded.

By preconcerted arrangement, I joined Mendez with fifteen riflemen, at midnight, at the *polvon*, or powder mills. Mendez had sixty lancers with him, who also carried arquebuses slung to their backs. Both bands were mounted, for we had to make a considerable detour in order to reach the hacienda unobserved by the enemy's outposts.

When sufficiently near the point of attack, we left our horses in charge of a small guard, and, descending into the dry bed of the *fosse*, or ravine, which ran along this side of the town, cautiously approached the gate of entrance to the hacienda, opposite to a *salleporte* in the wall of the town, by which reinforcements could be sent to the aid of the place, whenever needed. It was evident that riflemen were desirable to prevent communication by this route between the hacienda and the plaza. The shrubbery would effectually conceal the smallness of our band.

To render our aim effective, however, daylight had to be waited for, and as we lay silently among the dry leaves, we heard the tread and frequent challenge of the sentry within the wall of the town and in the guard-house at the hacienda, the light from which was plainly seen.

Mendez' force, with the stealth and silence of Indians, approached the entrance to the hacienda, and, at the first gleam of dawn, fell upon the guard on duty, thus gaining an entrance before the entire force, which was about equal to their own, could be brought against them. The attack upon the hacienda rudely disturbed the quiet of the hour of dawn. The noise of strife and clash of arms were quickly succeeded by a long roll from the plaza, the response to the order to "fall in." This was the signal that our turn to take part in the combat was approaching. Foreseeing the necessity for coolness, precision of aim, and complete concealment of the smallness of our numbers, I cautioned the men on these points, and we awaited in silence the coming of the enemy.

Suddenly the iron gate to the *salle-porte* went up with a clang, and two by two the white-ribboned soldiers, trailing arms, stepped through, and began deploying in the front, with the regularity of a dress parade.

The saying that "all is fair in war," is equivalent to saying that all is equally fair in an unfair procedure. War is, by the novelist, and often by the historian, made to appear attractive, and doubtless the pomp and panoply serve the purpose of blinding the reason, for the moment, to its unmitigated savagery. But to the actor in the strife, who may be capable of analyzing the motives and traits exhibited, it is not difficult to agree with the philosophy which suggests man's bestial origin.

We directed a steady fire at short range into the ranks of the enemy, reloading, and firing again. The unexpected ambush and precision of aim threw them instantly into confusion. They had no means of judging of our numbers, but the sharpness of the reports and fatality of aim, advised them that they were under fire of the dreaded rifles, and they retreated within the gate, leaving their dead and wounded on the field.

The momentary shock which our unexpected fire had produced was followed by a brisk fire from the walls, and a rain of bullets followed which would have exterminated us, had not each man sought such shelter as tree or rock afforded. This furious fire brought a squad from the soldiers of Mendez to our assistance, but, as the enemy made no attempt to storm our position, the reinforcement was not needed. After awhile the fire from within the walls slackened, a proof to me that some new method of attack was being devised.

Meantime the firing at the hacienda had ceased, and the soldiers informed us that Mendez had won a complete victory over the garrison. I felt sure that our position could not long remain tenable, cut off as we were by distance from our army and within the lines of the enemy, and determined to draw my men out of the ravine and join Mendez preparatory to the necessary withdrawal of our united force; it being no part of the plan in these forays to attempt to hold any ground longer than was necessary to accomplish that destruction which was the main object of the expedition. By making a feint on a point in the wall at a little distance, I succeeded in distracting the enemy's attention sufficiently to unable us to scramble out of the moat and join Mendez at the hacienda.

The scene before us on entering the court of the estate was decidedly dramatic, but I felt that the situation demanded my intervention.

The various offices and outbuildings surrounding the court were ablaze, and the rich cargoes of cacao and other merchandise, which, with the destruction of the buildings, had been the object of the expedition, were being strapped on the backs of mules preparatory to being carried off for the uses of our commissariat.

So far the instincts of the old soldier had led Mandez to accomplish the legitimate business in hand with celerity. On such occasions moments are of great value; the enemy's advantages of numbers and positions were so great, that as much sagacity and calculation were required to get away before they could block the avenues of retreat, as in any other part of the undertaking.

Having, however, got the business under way, Mendez had yielded to his baser instincts, and was inflicting what mischief he could upon those who had fallen into his hands.

Dead soldiers, wearing the red as well as the white, lay scattered on the pavement of the court. Evidently the place had not been yielded without a severe struggle. What, however, instantly claimed my attention, was a group beneath a large mango tree in a corner of the court. Conspicuous among the men stood Mendez, a colored handkerchief bound round his head, his coat thrown off, and holding in his hand his long Toledo sword, the blade of which was wet with blood. He was directing some soldiers who were trying to cast the end of a rope over a branch of the tree, the other end being fastened by a slip-noose round the neck of one of the prisoners. A similiar preparation was being made not far off to hang another of the prisoners, most of whom were on their knees muttering payers for that mercy from their God which had been denied them by their fellow-man.

Mendez' sense of his duty to get away at once from a dangerous position was evidently struggling with his desire for vengeance and hatred of his enemies. He was urging the men to greater haste, and not without reason, for the bullets of the enemy's skirmishers were raining about the place in a way calculated to convince us that they must be backed by a considerable force. As capture in this war had the most terrible significance, it behooved us to break through the net fast closing around us. All of my instincts of humanity and sense of manhood, however, revolted against this mode of dealing with defenceless prisoners, and as my men were well in hand while those of Mendez were much scattered, I determined to effect by a *coup de main* that which there was neither time nor opportunity to accomplish by less arbitrary means. At a word from me the Americans walked up to the prisoners, and, casting the ropes from their necks, took possession of them, while turning to Mendez, whom I saluted formally, I told him I could not consent to the barbarism he contemplated.

His answer, fire flashing from his eye, was a lunge with his sword at my breast. Before I had acted, however, I had foreseen consequences and was prepared. My rifle was instantly at my shoulder, and the Colonel's foot was as instantly arrested. I confess that I was strongly tempted to send a bullet through his heart. His savage expression gradually softened, and, as he dropped the point of his sword, he said I should account to him later, but that, at present, we had to get away.

The latter necessity was indeed apparent, for some of the men were already engaged in repelling the enemy from the gate of the enclosure, and we now turned a resolute front upon them, forcing them back with resistless impetuosity. Then mounting the horses which had been brought to the hacienda, Mendez, with the cargoes, and the prisoners, whom I had turned over to a trusty native sergeant whom I knew, stole away by a devious route from the dangerous locality. Having foreseen the difficulties of the retreat, and knowing that the native lancers would be most serviceable both in guarding the plunder and in leading the way, I hastily told Mendez that, if they would take care of our horses, I would take care of the rear, which was most exposed to attack by the enemy. The old soldier's wrinkled face expanded into a smile as he acquiesced in the arrangement. He probably felt that, although the "*Estrangeros*," as we were sometimes called, had queer notions regarding the treatment of captives, they were all right where fighting was to be done. The enemy pressed us hard, and if the riflemen had not been in the rear to check their advance, disaster must have resulted. After harassing us for about a mile, and finding that reinforcements were coming to our aid, they withdrew.

Four of the riflemen were killed or subsequently died of wounds received in this affair, and Mendez after the service we rendered in securing his safe withdrawal from the hacienda, laughed away the little unpleasantness between us. Indeed, he afterwards humorously satirized it in one of his improvisations, enacting the part of the "New Don Quixote," to the great amusement of his audience. As his savagery was not generally approved in the camp, I received many tokens of approval for the lesson I had given him.

CHAPTER V.

Visit of the American Minister—Truce declared, for the occasion only—Major Dorse's insidious treachery—An affair in the suburbs—Death of Dorse—Cholera and other sickness—Radicate's fiasco—I form a native company of riflemen—Assigned to the "post of honor."

THE arrival about this time, at the camp, of the United States Minister and suite was an interesting event.

In order to observe strict neutrality, a ceremonial visit was made to Chamorro, in the plaza, and afterwards to the commanding officer representing the Democratic government, in the Jalteva. A truce, the first during the war, was agreed upon for the occasion. Ostensibly the purport of the visit was to convey the good-will and greeting of the republic in the north to the sister republic in Central America. Some of us, however, knew that the sympathy of the people of a representative government like that of the United States was naturally with the cause of the people in Nicaragua.

The practical importance and significance of the visit to the Democrats was expressed by the presence, in the suite of the Minister, of two emissaries of Colonel William Walker, of California. Captain Hornsby and Mr. Du Brissott were empowered by Colonel Walker to contract with the Democratic government for the service of himself and such agriculturists as he might bring with him—all to become naturalized citizens of Nicaragua, and to receive certain grants of land and other emoluments, as consideration for their intention of developing the natural resources of the country. And they were furthermore, in view of the unsettled condition of affairs, to be permitted to come armed for purposes of self-defence.

This permission would presumably exempt them from molestation from the United States authorities at San Francisco, who might, without it, detain them as invaders of the peace of a neighboring nation.

The terms were accepted and the agreement was confirmed by the government at Leon, and constituted the authority under which Colonel Walker and his adherents subsequently acted.

The epithet *filibuster*, by which the British

sought to bring discredit on a movement which bade fair to destroy their time-honored privilege of dominating the affairs of the comparatively feeble governments of the West India Islands and Central America, was echoed by the anti-slavery party in the United States, and thus Britannia continues to rule, except where the French are acquiring the right to the Isthmus. The next step towards possession will be taken when an Anglo-German commercial alliance shall purchase of Nicaragua the proper concession for an interoceanic canal across the only feasable route for that purpose. And then the respective foreign governments will find it necessary to ensure observance of the vested rights of their citizens by a protectorate that will culminate in an occupation of the adjacent territory.

Meantime the *statesmen* of the United States will quote the Monroe doctrine, but will be chiefly active in seeking the Presidential succession for themselves.

The unusual opportunity afforded by the truce, for an interchange of news and greetings between relatives and former friends now divided by armed faction, drew crowds to the barriers, and as I learned that Major Dorse was among the foremost, I followed in the same direction.

The unaccustomed sound, and in loud tones, of the English language, drew me to a locality where I found Dorse, in the true stump-orator style, declaiming in the presence of the riflemen, the subject of his remarks being to set forth the superior advantages of the service of the Church party,—extending, in fact, an invitation to desert. I ordered the riflemen back to their quarters, and informed the crowd, who were naturally suspicious, of the nature of the Texan's oratory, so that they hooted him away. I thought no more of this incident at the time, looking upon it as a part of the natural impudence and audacity of Dorse. The next day, the short truce being over, a crumpled note, addressed in English, to the "Captain California," was handed me by the General's adjutant, which, on opening, I found to be from Dorse, thanking me for my ready acceptance of his propositions, and suggesting that in the next opportunity, offered by any of the numerous partial engagements of outposts, I should come over with the riflemen as agreed to, etc. The adjutant said the letter had been found wrapped tightly about the head of an arrow which had been projected over the barriers during the night.

I lost no time in seeking Jerez, on whom I burst with very little ceremony, and as the audience-chamber was filled with officers, many of whom greeted my approach with broad grins and laughter, I demanded of the General, as I glanced rather fiercely at them, whether there were any there who perchance supposed me capable of the action implied by the precious missive I bore in my hand, the contents of which I perceived they were acquainted with. I was rather young and impulsive in those days. They all, the General included, roared with laughter, mitigating the apparent rudeness, however, by one and all assuring me of their confidence in my good faith.

This attempt of Dorse to excite distrust of us among the native officers was perhaps no worse morally than any other *ruse de guerre*. But it was resented by the men, and I am afraid by me, with a feeling of vindictiveness that at a more mature age I could not have entertained. And each one of us resolved that on the first opportunity he would endeavor to square accounts with the wily Texan. Fate had decreed that the occasion should not be far distant.

The exploits of detached parties continued to keep alive the spirit of enterprise, and to give opportunity for distinction to those who sought more excitement than was afforded by the frequent light skirmishes at the barriers.

A suburb of the town, covered with thatched cottages and an occasional more substantial adobe structure, which had hitherto been, until recently, neutral ground, was now occupied by a force of the enemy, who met any feeble attempts of ours to investigate their proceedings with so lively a firing that we very soon desisted from disturbing them. All doubt of their object was set at rest when, one morning early, they opened, from an angle left unguarded by us, a cannonade upon our headquarters that threatened a speedy demolition of the Church as well as of the contiguous quarters of the soldiers. Colonel Olivas at once called for volunteers for a storming party. and the rifles were the first to offer.

In an hour five hundred men were on the way to the exposed position, and as, excepting for a little brush, the road was quite unsheltered, detachments starting from two different points rivalled each other in the effort to get on the ground first. Our movement was plainly seen from the plaza, reinforcements were sent to the battery, and we had the prospect of a lively fight. As we neared the point of attack, we encountered a brisk fire of grape and musketry, and the nature of the ground being very uneven, order was abandoned. Each man emulated his neighbor in his efforts to close in upon the enemy, so that, after a short run, we were too close to suffer from the fire of the field-pieces, and the struggle became a hand-to-hand conflict.

This lasted a short time only, and then each partial protection against the rain of bullets, whether a cane cottage whose walls offered no obstruction to their passage, or the more substantial adobe structure, was hastily sought as a rallying point, whence again to charge *en masse*.

As fast as we dislodged the enemy from one point they appeared at another. Bullets swept the air from every direction, and the opposing combatants were so mingled as to offer no distinguishing mark except that afforded by the color of the ribbons and facings of their uniforms. Dorse and all his men were there, their whiter skins and more European costumes rendering them easily distinguishable, as doubtless our riflemen were by them. Dorse himself had more nearly assimilated his dress to that of the native officers, though I caught two or three transient glimpses of him, but the rapidity of the changes of movement gave little opportunity for a steady aim.

Sad havoc was, however, being made, considering the not large number engaged, and when, after nearly an hour's hard fighting, we found ourselves in possession of the ground, the considerable space over which we had fought was literally covered with the dead. Red and white ribbons were apparently in about equal proportion.

The proximity of the enemy to the plaza had probably been an inducement for them to give way, as once within the walls they were assured of shelter from our shot. But as a rally in greater force was sure to follow, we set about firing every house and combustible thing that, if left, might afford them shelter. It was too far from our supporting lines for us to attempt to hold the place. When the work of demolition was complete, we drew our remaining force away and returned. Half of my little squad of riflemen was killed in this encounter, and nearly a third of the native troops with which we set out was also missing.

Among the disasters suffered by the enemy was the death of Major Dorse. He had fought with his accustomed valor, repeatedly encouraging his party to hold their ground. Three rifle-balls, at different times during the fight, had pierced his body, none of them proving immediately fatal. When, on their retreat, he was conveyed within their lines, and his life was slowly ebbing away, he, with characteristic pride, asked for his rifle. It was brought and held while he, with fading sight, tried to hit a mark. Such was the story brought us afterwards.

I shall spare myself and the reader the relation of many affairs of similar import which occurred during these summer months while my men dwindled in numbers, owing to the accidents of battle and the consumption of exceedingly bad whiskey. My good fortune at this time seemed to exempt me from harm from bullets—an immunity that subsequent experiences taught me was purely accidental. I was initiated, too, in a curious phase of state policy that would have disillusioned me of the "sacredness of the most glorious cause," etc., if that process had not already been completed. The loss of so many of my riflemen had thrown me for employment among the natives, with whose leaders I had consequently formed a more intimate acquaintance, and, as the enemy had suffered equally with ourselves from the various causes already enumerated, it seemed to me that the time had come for a bold and well-concerted movement to capture the plaza. We knew all about their relaxation of discipline and enterprise, not only through spies, but also from the fact that the "*Tierras muertes,*" as they were called,—the open ground exposed to the enemy's shot,—could now be traversed with impunity, while formerly the adventurous passenger would have been greeted by a rain of bullets. Filled with this idea, I sought a private audience with Generals Guerrero and Jerez, and urged that a picked band of men should make the assault, which, if properly conducted, could not fail of success.

Guerrero, the wily cabinet counsellor, after imposing secrecy, informed me that it would not at present suit the government at Leon to end the war; the effect, he said, would be to throw various claimants for office and emoluments—now happily employed in the field—upon the President, who could not possibly satisfy them all. New dissensions would therefore arise more difficult to treat than the single obstacle of the enemy in the plaza. The revelation was to me as discouraging probably as was the state of things which caused the despairing Roman to declare that "virtue is but a name." Music and revelry became the order in the camp. Fandangos, serenades, and gayety generally prevailed, while the hospitals were crowded with maimed and dying soldiers.

The Asiatic cholera came with a suddenness and violence that was in part due to the deficiency in sanitary regulations.

Those killed in the numerous skirmishes in the vicinity of the town were left to the buzzards, who, although constantly hovering in the air in vast throngs, were yet unable wholly to dispose of the harvest of food which war and pestilence combined cast out for them. The labor of interment was considered too heavy a task to impose upon the soldiers, and the habit of shooting all prisoners—indulged in by both sides—left us without that resource for a labor contingent. The custom that prevailed was to place the corpses of those who die at night, from whatever cause, upon the front-door steps every morning at sunrise. At this hour carts were driven along the principal streets, and the bodies, being collected, were conveyed to a cliff near the *Polvon*, about a mile outside the town, and there cast over, becoming soon a mass of putrefaction, the gases from which tainted the air we breathed. My health, which held good under conditions that had prostrated feeble and robust alike, now gave way.

An attack of brain-fever prostrated me. Weeks passed before I was able to take note of affairs going on in the camp, and then I found that on account of the pestilence hostilities had been suspended. They were resumed gradually as the cholera abated.

To any one capable of forecasting, the result of our supine inactivity appeared inevitable. The exchequer of each party was equally low, but the enemy had the advantage of drawing supplies from near home, in the defence of which they considered conscription and forced levies legitimate. On the other hand, our strength in men and means was derived from the distant department of Leon, and we were dependent upon volunteers for filling up our thinned ranks. As many of the men who had enlisted for short terms were getting tired, now that the novelty had worn off, and were, moreover, desirous of returning home for the replanting of their fields, we saw our force dwindling daily. So it became evident that our evacuation of the Jalteva would very soon be a necessity apparent to all.

In this condition of our affairs, in order to hide our weakness we sometimes assumed a bluster before the enemy.

Hence Colonel Radicate, our Italian chief of artillery, who was chiefly conspicuous for deficiency in the knowledge of engineering so necessary in his branch of the service, set about the erection of a trestle-work. After carrying this up to a height of forty feet he purposed to mount upon it heavy cannon from which to throw round shot into the plaza. He and I had been unfriendly for some time; the enmity was on his part, for I had too great a contempt for the man's lack of ability and moral character to regard him with any deeper feeling than dislike. As, however, his structure created considerable comment and expectation in the camp, General Pineda, Don Justo Lugo, and I, made an informal visit of inspection to it one evening. It was to be completed that night and the cannonade from it opened on the enemy at daylight the next morning.

We did not hesitate to pronounce it a trap that would be more fatal to its occupants than to the enemy, telling Radicate that the recoil of his heavy guns would shake it down; besides, that on so fragile a structure he could oppose no adequate resistance to the return shot of the enemy. We tried to dissuade him from making the experiment, failing in which, I believe I offended him by a censure which it was certainly not my place to make. His resentment took a shape I had not foreseen. An hour or two later I was accosted by an adjutant from the General, directing me to send such riflemen as were fit for duty to report to Colonel Radicate at daylight for service on the platform. Mendez and Don Justo were with me when the order came, and, as I could not contest it nor send men on a duty I had declared suicidal without accompanying them, I prepared for the morning's duty under a battery of jokes from my friends. One recommended an umbrella attachment to enable me to alight easily, and the other the padding of my clothing to the same end, all promising to see me decently buried, etc.

In the morning I found Radicate waiting for daylight. The guns were pointed and all ready as I quietly took my place with three riflemen on the platform.

No public work like this of Radicate's could be carried on in the cantonment without minute details of its progress and probable purpose being conveyed to the enemy through the numerous spies. Therefore, it was reasonable to infer that the enemy were as ready for their part in the tragic farce as we ourselves. We had only to wait a short time for the first faint rays of daylight to direct the guns on the quartels or barracks in the plaza; then we fired. The unstable structure actually rocked with the recoil; the cross timbers were not fastened to each other, and a few such shocks must inevitably have set them sliding: but we were not destined to go down by that method, for immediately two or three round shots screamed over our heads, and then, while our Colonel was remedying some displacement of the timbers caused by the recoil of our guns, a twenty-four pound shot struck the trestle under our feet, the splinters flying in all directions. What followed I have a very vague idea of. It seemed as if we were being pounded by a trip-hammer in full swing. I found myself scrambling away from the débris of the trestle, which was scattered all over the earth, and as I was not much hurt, I was soon ready to join my friends and the spectators generally in the uproarious merriment which the ridiculous fiasco evoked.

It was strange that, though the demolition of the structure was complete, very little personal damage had been done, either by shot or falling guns and timbers. To those of us who had any knowledge of affairs at head-quarters, it became apparent about this time that some important movement was in contemplation. Our condition forbade any possibly successful aggressive action, and one alternative only remained—namely, the evacuation of our present position.

One morning, after reporting at head-quarters, in answer to a summons from the Commanding General, I was requested by Jerez to select from the different companies in the cantonment sixty of the most expert marksmen, and form with them a company of native riflemen.

I had no difficulty in obtaining the requisite number of volunteers willing to exchange the musket and a native commander for a rifle and service under "*El Capitan California.*" As I selected the best soldiers, though naturally against the will of their officers, I got together a very efficient body of men.

When I received General Jerez' orders to form this company, he told me that a very responsible service would soon devolve on me, for which he desired me to have reliable men. This special service was to take command of the rearguard with my own and the company of Captain Chevas in the evacuation of the cantonment.

I felt honored by the distinction. The rear would be the only point exposed to the assault of the enemy, who would doubtless harass a force abandoning its position. I suggested to General Guerrero that one hundred and twenty men was a scanty allowance for this duty. He replied that as every resource which they could muster would be necessary for the successful attack which they purposed making on the town of Massaya, about eighteen miles distant, garrisoned by a strong force of the enemy, he hoped I would do my best with my two companies. "*Es el Pueste de honor mi Capitan*," said the wily old chief, who well knew how to make an effectual appeal to the pride of youth; and although I would rather have had more men even at the expense of some honor, I bowed acquiescence.

CHAPTER VI.

Evacuation of the cantonment at Granada—Severe fighting and loss in my company—A Bongo cruise on Lake Managua—An earthquake—Arrival at Leon—Amusements and gayety.

IT was near daylight before we accomplished the tedious process of getting the ordnance and commissariat stores, together with the impedimenta and camp followers, under way. Then I could relinquish the position held all night, in order to check the skirmishing attempts of the enemy trying to find out whether our move indicated a real evacuation, or was merely a feint for the purpose of making an assault on their beloved plaza.

When I finally gave the welcome order to file into the Massaya road, the pale streaks of approaching dawn were visible in the eastern sky.

We had barely reached the Campo Santo, a mile outside the town, when the halt of the mass of women and children constituting the wives and families of the soldiers, and of the various camp followers, blocked the road ahead. By sending to ascertain the cause of delay, I found that the heavy artillery, which Radicate, with his usual injudiciousness, was endeavoring to convey over muddy roads, was stuck fast.

An hour's unsuccessful effort at releasing it was wasted, and then the cannon were spiked and abandoned. Meantime the main body, by pushing on toward Massaya, had satisfied the enemy of the object of the movement, so that they turned their attention to reinforcing Massaya and harassing our retreat. As the country through which we were marching was a swamp, over which a corduroy road offered the only means of passage for a body of troops in support of Massaya, their efforts to break through the slender barrier became furious. In the scanty forest my soldiers were able partially to protect themselves from the shower of bullets which flew thick after us, and the narrow pass helped me to hold my own against superior numbers.

In this way we continued, fighting and slowly falling back, during most of the day. The beams of the torrid sun poured on our heads and added to the exhaustion necessarily resulting from the great activity required to keep the constantly pressing enemy in check. I had to be wherever the attack was hardest, and seemed doomed to fall, so constant was my exposure. Hoping against hope for reinforcements, requests for which I had repeatedly sent, we fought doggedly through the weary hours. Near Massaya the ground was higher, and the enemy sought, by passing around us, to succor their garrison, which the sound of heavy firing ahead told us was engaged with our main body. The relief we obtained by the enemy's lateral movement to the support of Massaya was counterbalanced by the exposure of our flank on the more open country. They were not slow to seize this advantage, and while repelling an assault here we temporarily left the road open in the rear. Of this we were speedily apprised by the screaming of women and musketry-fire in their direction. Hastening back, we found the enemy shooting and bayoneting the dense throng of frightened and defenceless women and children, whose bodies, arrayed in poor finery, their long, dishevelled tresses trailing in the dust, were a sad addition to the day's slaughter. We quickly came up with them, still engaged in their dastardly work, and I venture to say that the fire we poured into them was more fatal than any they had before received.

We soon had the road to ourselves, and were joined by the remnant of the miserable camp people.

The movement necessary for forcing the enemy back from our flank, and the steady advance of the main body had completely isolated us from our army, of whose position we could judge only by the firing in the distance.

The ground was now a wide plain, sufficiently overgrown with shrubs to conceal an enemy, and as I only had about fifty men left out of the two companies with which I had left Granada, it seemed to me wise to await approaching darkness rather than, by attempting to march in daylight, draw attention to the smallness of my force.

We were indeed a forlorn remnant. The tremendous physical exertions I had undergone, combined with such intense thirst that my swollen tongue actually refused utterance, compelled me to seek a temporary rest. Some of the poor women whom we had rescued from the slaughter, seeing my great need of a drink of water, offered to go to a group of houses at a little distance in search of some, although the chance of falling into an ambush of the enemy was very great. This I at first would not permit, but finally consented to by accompanying them. We found plenty of water and no enemy.

No sooner had night fallen than we moved towards the town. The firing had ceased some time before, and as no triumphant peal of bells had rung out, we knew that the Democrats had failed to capture the place. Some of the women were familiar with the environs, and with their aid I endeavored to reach the Managua road, rightly guessing that Jerez would place himself on that side of the enemy which would give him communication with Leon. The light skirmish fire and the barking of dogs soon indicated to us the course of our troops. It was near midnight when we encountered our outposts, the army having gone into camp on the Managua road. We were admitted within the lines, and as I wished to avoid the chance of having a guard detail made from my greatly fatigued men, I deferred reporting my arrival, directing the men to sleep on their arms.

So profound was my sleep, although my

bed was the bare ground, that I was only awakened by the notes of the reveillé, and, as I found a general preparation for marching going on, I reported my arrival to the officer of the day. While the men were preparing such breakfast as the exigencies of the situation permitted, I called on General Jerez, who expressed himself highly pleased at the persistence with which the rear-guard had kept the enemy back, and did not seem surprised at the heavy loss sustained.

I found that no further attempt was to be made on Massaya, indeed the demonstration of the previous day had been more a feint to draw the enemy's attention from the real object, which was to return to Leon. By abandoning for the present the oriental and meridional departments of Granada and Rivas, the Democrats assured themselves of the sovereignty over the rest of the State, with the fair hope that the prevalence of popular ideas would ultimately produce a reconciliation with the claims of the opposing faction.

The march was resumed with the adjuncts of music and flying colors, intended as an indication that we were only going away because we wanted to, and that if the enemy was disposed to knock the chip from our shoulders, we were ready to give them a chance. They, however, were content, and probably glad to let us depart unmolested, and we soon reached the shore of Lake Managua, where it was decided to embark the artillery and heavy stores on a fleet of bongos, awaiting us at that place.

During the fight on the previous day, a musket ball, which had been deflected from my leg by the scabbard of my sword, had produced a bruise which at the time I had paid no attention to; it was now painful and my leg swollen, and as some of the wounded were going to be sent in the bongos, I asked permission to accompany them. This was readily granted, and I secured a place for my blankets and myself between two brass field-pieces, the cargo of a large canoe or bongo, in preference to herding with the wounded soldiers, in a more commodious craft.

As the picturesque line of marching soldiers filed along the road skirting the shore of the lake, to the inspiring strains of martial music, our bongos and launches spread their sails to the gentle breeze that wafted us over the peaceful bosom of the lake. Peaceful we soon found, near the shores only, for though the breeze was only moderate, the swell further out was too heavy for our fragile and overladen craft, and the boatmen were fain to skirt the shore rather than trust the stronger winds of the middle of the lake.

The change from the dust and fatigue of the march, and the reaction of rest and quiet, as well as safety, made the repose doubly grateful to me. I enjoyed the lazy motion of the canoe, and the quaint songs of the boatmen, as we glided near the vine-draped crags or sandy coves.

So quiet was our progress along these emerald shores, that I often shot the *pavo del monte*, or tufted wild turkey, and the wild guinea fowl, as they sought their food among the dry leaves, or rested on the lower branches of the trees by the water. At night, when we hauled the bongos on the beach, the supper was prepared by the fire lighted on the sand, and as we had ample provision of chocolate, plantains, and other vegetables, with the wild birds I had shot, our fare was of the best. The peacefulness of the repose beneath the spangled heavens, where no dread sound of war's alarm was apprehended, was peculiarly pleasant to my wearied condition of mind and body. I could fully appreciate that luxurious inertness, which is the normal condition of the uneducated Central American.

In the early morning the wind was usually a little fresh, then we hugged the shore, or sought a sheltered cove, and tied up until the wind moderated. Thus, on the second afternoon of our voyage we landed for the night at the foot of the volcano, Monotombito. As the sun was still high in the heavens, I climbed the steep mountain-side, over blocks of scoria and lava, which afforded a passage-way, rough, but less fatiguing than that of the loose, soft ashes above them.

As the labor of climbing produced great pain in my swollen knee, I had to give it up, and return to the boats. The next morning we arrived at the *debarcadero*, where carts with oxen attached were awaiting to receive our heavy cargoes.

Here we began a slow progress through the woods around the base of the mighty volcano, Monotombo, whose extinct prototype I had partially ascended on the previous day.

The lurid fires from the crater of this volcano illumined by night the sky above, and was visible at vast distances.

Warnings of the hidden force pent up within had been frequent of late, in slight shiverings of the earth and the ejection of ashes and vapor. It was my fortune to witness an extraordinary exhibition of its power, more violent than any for many years. The long line of carts was winding along the forest road, whose soft surface gave forth no sound beneath the broad wheels, which were simple sections of the trunks of trees, bored through the centre to admit the wooden axle. The friction of these axles, when not lubricated, as was the custom, with the bark of some gum-exuding tree, caused sounds the reverse of melodious. The monkeys and forest birds seemed to vie in their vocal efforts with this discordant sound, so that our advent in these domains of savage nature greatly disturbed its normal quiet. I was reclining on my blankets, which had been arranged on some gun-carriages in one of the carts, when I became conscious of a sudden cessation of the usual accompaniment of sound and motion. Something seemed to have cast a spell over the scene.

The long file of men and oxen had come to a sudden halt. Silence succeeded to the various noises of the march and of the forest denizens. The men, who had been driving the oxen and beguiling the way with the usual objurgations which the Spanish *carretero* deems fit for the efficient service of his calling, as stimulant to the dumb beast, were on their knees in the road, hat in hand, busily muttering prayers to their favorite saints. I scarcely comprehended the meaning of the scene until the variously muttered words "*un tremblor*" and the slight shivering of the cart apprised me that the dreaded earthquake was upon us. The motion increased to a violent shaking and then to a heaving like the billows of the ocean. As the shaking became more violent, the fall of numerous decayed and unstable trees and branches in the surrounding forest bore evidence to the extent of the disturbance, while the swaying of the living trees in the calm air was testimony to its force.

The wave passed along and—it was gone.

The oxen, without orders, resumed their slow pace; the drivers renewed their various expletives to urge them to greater speed, and the creaking of the wheels blended again with the scream of monkey and parrot. An earthquake was of too common occurrence in this land of the sun and fire to create any impression after the danger was over. But for three days thereafter the volcano poured forth ashes that literally covered the plain of Leon over an area of hundreds of miles, so that the landscape had the wintry appearance of fallen snow.

When I arrived at Leon the troops were already there. Although they had not been successful in vanquishing the Church oligarchy, they had circumscribed their rule within the limits of the oriental department and such localities as were accessible by lake navigation, the facilities for which were not possessed by the Democrats. Their reception was, in consequence, an ovation. Although a foreigner, being a survivor of the little band of strangers that had done good service in the cause, my welcome by the kindly Leonese was cordial in the extreme. The fine house and grounds of a padre, whose estate had been sequestrated because of his adherence to the party of Granada, were assigned for my use and for those other Americans who had served in the army.

In the arborescent court of this fine mansion, where the water of a fountain sparkled in the sunlight, and hammocks were fastened between the trees, I enjoyed a period of repose, delightful after the excitement and fatigue incident to the life in the army.

Many weeks I passed in this pleasant retreat. Leon was gay, after the fashion of Spanish-American gayety.

The guitar and marimbo were in great request.

The impassioned *improvisatore* sang and twanged his instrument beneath the balconies, and the *baile*, in its varieties of cachuco, fandango, and bolera, was danced in hall and under the moon's pale light.

Horseback riding is here the only means of locomotion outside the city—at least for the young, who do not care for the slow, canopied ox-cart in which elderly ladies sometimes smoke their cigaritos and chat while being conveyed to and fro between the distant haciendas and the town. So riding is common alike to women and children, who, when not riding *en pillon* with a gentleman, use the short stirrups and sit astride the horse's back, as do the Arabs, and who from constant practice become very accomplished.

As Leon and its vicinity was the home of many of the friends I had made in the army, I was at no loss for society, and shared in all amusements. Then Leon in itself was very beautiful. Characterized by a friar chronicler of the olden time as " A Mahomet's Paradise." Also famed for the beauty of its Moorish architecture, and especially for the loveliness of its natural surroundings.

From the roof of its Cathedral of Saint Peter, which has sustained the shock of recoil from a battery of thirty pieces of artillery during that dread siege of 1823, when "a thousand houses were burned in a single night," can be seen in one view thirteen volcanoes!—a view in many respects unequalled for variety and grandeur in the world.

The noble cathedral, built at a cost of five million dollars when labor was valued at about a shilling a day, was completed in thirty-seven years, and has retained for a hundred and fifty years its strength and beauty of outline. One tower was indeed riven by lightning, which did not damage the body of the church. These reminiscences of that reposeful life at Leon, contrasting so vividly with the eventful experiences at Granada, have blended in one picture seen in the vista of departed years.

Thought reverts to that time, and I seem to

hear the peal from that old campanile in the church at Granada ; the *feu de joie* of the cannon, the clash of cymbals, and *fanfare* of trumpets—the semi-barbaric Moorish music. Then appears the long procession of mitred and surpliced clergy passing between walls of soldiery, whose colors are veiled in honor of a Church that oppresses them on earth, perhaps, but holds the heritage of paradise for true believers. Thanks are to be rendered to the Most High for victories in a people's cause, for the Church is wise as well as powerful, and lends her countenance to all parties who are faithful.

There stands the thrice gallant Jerez, the chivalrous Valle, the noble Pineda. Where are they now?

And where the careless heart that beat responsive to high impulse—to reckless daring?

The purple haze still lifts from the lake as of old. The birds sing in the tropic forest, and the flowers bloom by the wayside. Nature smiles as serenely as ever. But man has his little day, and then " he is seen no more forever." And so with man's works.

Lizards now bask in the mellow sunshine on the ruined walls of Granada. There came a day when the fair and picturesque city, whose antique, sun-embrowned, Moresco architecture had so long reflected the tropic sun-rays, and given back the moon's pale beams in softer light, and whose hardened cement seemed to defy the slow assaults of time, crumbled before the blows of the sapper and the blast of the mine. *"Aqui fue Granada"*—" Here was Granada"—wrote General Henningsen over the ruins he had made, when his gallant band of heroes could no longer hold the place against the overwhelming numbers of the enemy. Forcing the armed cordon which surrounded them, they left behind but a barren victory.

But these are the tales of unsung heroism. The world is full of such, and he was a wise man who said :

" Nothing succeeds like success."

CHATER VII.

El Tamarinda—Trip to Honduras—Return to Leon—Arrival of General Muños—Vacillating policy—Advent of the "Filibusters"—Their impressions of the country—Jarring councils—Military expedition to the Department Meridional—Night march—Capture of enemy's picket.

THE extensive estate of my friend General Don Mateo Pineda included that part of the sea-coast known as *El Tamarinda*, renowned for its surf-bathing facilities, situated about twenty miles from Leon. I was included in the party composed of his family and friends invited to make a camping excursion to this favorite spot. As the journey was to be made on horseback, the provisions, camp equipage, and servants going on the day before in carts, some of us were anxious to know what particular lady would be assigned to our special protection on the way. Many of the young ladies rode *en pillon* with a gentleman friend instead of alone. The friend was chosen by a parent or relation of the demoiselle. I was, therefore, flattered when the General requested me to escort his niece, a lively miss of some sixteen summers, who carried a much beribboned guitar over her shoulder. As the gayly equipped cavalcade rode through the streets it was pleasant to notice the cordial and affectionate greetings of the populace, the gentlemen of the party being almost without exception military chiefs in the army. Passing through the suburb of Subtiaba, which still contains the idols and carved work of that ancient semi-civilization which pre-dated the founding of Leon in 1610, we were soon on the open plain which extended to the coast, whose sand dunes were visible in the distance.

As we had started late in the afternoon, the moon illuminated our way across the sandy waste bordering the sea, the beat of whose surf had been for some time audible before we caught a view of the flashing breakers. Then the bright blaze of the camp fire and the savory odor of cooking viands greeted our senses, and as our ride of twenty miles had prepared us to do justice to the good things awaiting us, we were soon seated on the white sand around the dried bullocks' hides on which was spread the ample feast,

Little ceremony is needed on these occasions, and I venture to say that a merrier party than ours is rarely gathered together.

Tall pines waved their fragrant canopies above us. The blazing fires and flashing spray illumined the scene, and the balmy air from the tropic sea refreshed us as it swept by. Then, after a stroll along the moonlit beach, our blankets were spread under the fragrant pines, 'neath the starry sky, and our sleep was lulled by the rhythmic beat of the surf.

The next day was devoted to the more permanent adjustments of the camp, as we purposed remaining a week or two. Poles were lashed from tree to tree and placed across; on these, pine boughs were thrown, making a shelter from the light dews and spray. As this was the dry season, no further protection was required for perfect comfort. The bathing was delightful, the water refreshing without chilling us.

I fancy that our life on this shore of the great Pacific Ocean—still fringed with the primeval forests—though unaccompanied by the thousand and one modern improvements considered by many as essentials of life, was more enjoyable, and certainly more restful, than that of the favored few whom it is the ambition of a majority of the world to emulate.

We bathed at break of day; no hardship, this, as the Central American has learned to utilize, for business and recreation, the pleasantest of the hours, the noontide being given up to repose. Chocolate and *biscoche*, a kind of sweet cake, made the early breakfast, a later one succeeding at ten o'clock, by which time I had generally "bagged" a deer, a wild turkey or two, or something equally adaptable to culinary uses.

After breakfast Pineda, Don Justo, the good Padre Jerez, who was also of the party, and myself, often discussed philosophical questions, in which Don Justo, considering the time and place, was not to be despised. Indeed, I was delighted to find, widely as I was separated by nationality and antecedents from these people, that not a few among the better educated were in accord with the advanced modern thought on the to me superlatively interesting topics which teach that "the proper study of mankind is man."

Our discussions often scandalized the good Padre—good in the best sense of the word, for he was ever found where suffering and want called for aid, on the battle-field regardless of personal danger, and equally so in the pestilence-visited hospitals, humble and unassuming, as was the Master whom he reverently served, but withal bigoted in favor of holy mother Church, whose waning power he assured us he never more regretted than when listening to the heretical discourse of Don Justo and myself, who he said were proper subjects for an *auto-da-fe*.

Argument was, of course out of the question with him, as his logic began and ended with the authoritative dogma which excluded the possibility of error from a Church, the keys of which had been handed to St. Peter, with the promise that what he and his successors should bind and loosen should be final. When I told him that his conclusions, considered as a sequence to his premises, were irrefutable, he seemed puzzled, but supposed that I was laughing at him.

Of course our time was varied with other amusements than philosophical discussion, guitar music and singing, cards, etc. Occasionally Mendez and Pineda would accompany me in my hunting excursions, which, to save fatigue, were usually made on horseback. Once we came upon a puma, or *tigre*, as he is there called. He was directly in the little bridle-path we were following through the shrubby growth of the vicinity.

"Look, *Capitan*," shouted Pineda, who chanced to be in advance. "*Mire el tigre!*" See the tiger. The beautiful spotted beast was standing in the path with head erect and tail gently waving from side to side, regarding us apparently with surprise mingled with fear. I was off my horse and had thrown my reata to Mendez in a moment, and as quickly the rifle was at my shoulder, but as the beast's head interfered with my aim at a vital spot, I waited a few moments until he slightly turned his gaze to one side, leaving his throat exposed, then I sent the fatal bullet to his heart.

Mendez was in raptures, and declared that he and the orderly who accompanied us would wait and save the fine skin of the animal, while Pineda and myself rode on. One of Mendez' peculiar tastes, which he could never get the rest of us to conform to in Granada, was a love for baked cats. He generally had a hand in the cooking, too, and after dinner on this day, when we were all smoking the inevitable cigarritos, he remarked in a casual way that he had noticed that Donna Pineda and Don Justo and El Capitan California had enjoyed the excellent hash. When we assented, he said he hoped we would now admit that our dislike for cat-diet had been prejudiced, for the hash was tiger-hash, ordering Chico at the same time to exhibit the great cat-like paw of the beast, as corroborative of his assertion. Of course we were all made sick by the revelation, but as Mendez was a licensed rough jester, we could do nothing with him.

I subsequently killed another of these beautiful animals, as well as numerous beasts and reptiles only seen in northern countries in the menageries. After two weeks of this life, during which we visited the contiguous estates and had a very enjoyable time, we returned to Leon. Finding that there was no immediate prospect for a renewal of operations against the enemy, I sought and obtained leave to visit the gold mines of the District of Olancho in Honduras, a hundred and fifty miles distant, whither two of my former riflemen, who had recovered convalescence in the quiet life at Leon, agreed to accompany me.

We started on horseback, a blanket and a little provision of fine groceries and a few simple cooking utensils being all that we required to supplement the hospitable fare we were sure to be provided with by the inhabitants by the way, to whom in those sparsely settled districts the advent of a traveller from the cities of the great world was a benefit conferred, far greater than any return in the shape of a night's lodging and food.

For two or three days after we left the great plain of Leon we rode through the woods, over the broad national roadway, made in the days of Spanish power. This road bore evidence in its general structure to the enterprise of that people, just as its utterly neglected condition testified to the degeneracy of their descendants.

After passing through the ancient and considerable town of Choluteca in Honduras, we had encamped for the night by the way-side on some elevated ground, chosen to avoid the insects which swarmed in the lower lands. Our supper of broiled venison, roasted plantains, and chocolate had been disposed of, and as we lay on our blankets near the bright fire which had served to cook our supper, we were startled by the familiar hail from out the darkness of the road "Quien vive." It proved to be Colonel Rubio of Honduras, whom I had known as belonging to the Honduras contingent in our army at Granada. He was travelling with a small escort from the President of Honduras to offer the Democratic government at Leon the diplomatic and military services of General Muñoz, now of Honduras, but formerly, I believe, of San Salvador, for the prosecution and settlement of the differences between the two factions in Nicaragua.

Muñoz, although he had failed on a former occasion in an attempt to overthrow the Nicaraguan government under the Presidency of Don Laureano Pineda—the father of my friend of that name,—was conceded on all hands to be the ablest soldier in Central America, so that it needed but little urging on Rubio's part to induce me to return, feeling sure that Muñoz's advent in Nicaragua would be the signal for a move upon the enemy. Accordingly we returned, and a few days thereafter were again installed in our old quarters in Leon.

General Muñoz's arrival seemed to stir up anew a military spirit. It did not, however, take long to disabuse the public mind of the hopes thus inspired. Wily as he was by nature, it was plain that his diplomacy had the one end in view, that of constituting himself the *tertium quid* or basis for the new government, in which he hoped the hostile factions would reconcile their differences. As soon as I saw his motive, I began to get ready again for the Honduras gold mines.

The fates which govern the fall of a leaf, as they do the affairs of men, were, however, preparing an element destined to change the vacillating character of the Democratic government.

In a former chapter I alluded to the presence in the suite of the American Minister who visited the hostile camps at Granada, of certain emissaries of Colonel William Walker, a man then prominently before the public on account of the unsuccessful armed invasion he had made on the Mexican provinces of Sonora and Lower California.

In consequence of the approval by the government at Leon of a certain contract with Walker for supplies of men, mentioned in the agreement, for obvious reasons, as emigrants, but in reality soldiers, Walker had sailed from San Francisco in the brig Vesta with fifty-six *emigrants*, composed of the most resolute and daring men that could be found willing to engage in so hazardous an enterprise as that of military service in a revolutionary army engaged in a war which was conducted on principles not recognized in civilized warfare.

My first intimation of their arrival was, when in response to a summons from President Castelloñ, he informed me that Walker had landed in the San Salvadorian port of *La Union*, but had re-embarked, and would enter the Nicaraguan harbor of Realejo probably during the day.

The President desired me, with Dr. Livingstone (ex-American Consul), and Colonel Ramirez of the army, to proceed to Realejo and convey to Walker and the Americans the welcome of the President of Nicaragua.

We arrived at Realejo on horseback, about midnight, and found the streets of that usually quiet village crowded with armed Americans, who, in true California style, were having things their own way. The *pulperias*, where *aguardiente* was sold, were doing a thriving business. This and the brusque, aggressive manners of the strangers was assurance to me that I was again among my countrymen.

Colonel Walker himself did not, at the time,

impress me as the man of indomitable will and energy which I afterwards found him to be. He was quiet and unassuming, " as mild a mannered man as ever cut a throat or scuttled ship."

A certain expression of the eye would, however, probably have indicated to a physiognomist the reserve of power veiled under so placid an exterior.

Although this narrative assumes to be personal only, yet a proper understanding of the historical events with which it is connected, makes it imperative that a certain criticism of the acts of others should accompany the story.

As General Walker has been regarded, almost more than any other man, from points of view differing very widely, it is proper that I should state in the beginning that, in spite of my admiration for this extraordinary man of wonderful energy, courage, and personal integrity, I yet was always opposed to the insatiable ambition and disregard of public or private rights which characterized his actions in the one dominant pursuit of his life—that is, the attainment of absolute political power.

With this explanation I shall proceed to detail events as they appeared to me with as little prejudice as possible. As henceforth the most prominent character in the affairs of the Nicaraguan state and Democratic army was that of Colonel Walker, a brief sketch of his career up to this period may not be out of place.

William Walker, whose family is of Scotch descent, was a native of Nashville, Tennessee, where he was born in the year 1824. His education, which was finished in the universities of Paris, included a knowledge of the French and Latin languages and the medical and legal professions.

In 1850 he emigrated to California and became editor of the *San Francisco Herald*. He had previously edited the *Crescent* of New Orleans. His first military exploit was to raise a band of men with which he invaded the Mexican states of Lower California and Sonora. The professed object of this expedition was to protect the people of Sonora against the depredations of the Apache Indians, which the Mexican government and that of the state itself had failed to do.

It is true that no authority from either of those governments had been obtained, and, in the light of Walker's subsequent career, we may easily see that the attainment of supreme power for himself was the spring of action, the restraining of the Apaches being entirely subsidiary. From various causes, which a less sanguine or less fearless man might have foreseen, but which it is foreign to the present narrative to set forth, the attempt was a complete failure. The contract of Walker's emissaries with the Nicaraguan government reached him about this time, and no renewal of the attempt was made.

Those, however, who see in the character of Colonel Walker the spirit of a mere buccaneer, fail utterly to comprehend his nature. His motive in seeking supreme power was not like Aaron Burr's; but, rather, like the first Napoleon, who indeed was his great exemplar, he conceived himself to be an instrument of destiny before whom all lesser influences must give way. This confidence in his destiny led him to disregard obstacles which might have deterred other men, and which in the end caused his downfall. A more conciliatory nature, one better adapted to conform to inevitable circumstances, joined with his splendid force of will and magnetism, would have accomplished the difficult task he undertook.

On the following morning Colonel Walker and Captains Hornsby and Crocker accompanied Doctor Livingstone and myself back to Leon. The strangers saw with surprise and delight the beautiful country through which we rode,—its forest a tangled mass of plants and flowers, with the majestic cones of a dozen volcanic peaks forming a background towering to the sky.

In the villages through which we passed the moss-covered cottages and gigantic cacti which served as fences, were evidences of antiquity and repose in striking contrast to the busy marts of trade to which they were accustomed.

About eight miles from Realejo we entered the ancient and considerable town of Chinendega, beyond which towers the tall cone of the volcano *El Viejo*—the old.

A hundred and fifty years had passed since the Spanish warrior colonists, aided by African and native Indian labor, had erected the massive walls and laid in cement those enduring pavements which to-day echoed to the tread.

The silver-toned bells, coeval with the ancient city, rang out their welcome for the strangers who came from afar to fight in the sacred cause of liberty.

When we arrived at Leon, President Castelloñ received Walker with cordiality and consideration. The President's knowledge of French was defective. Walker at that time did not speak Spanish at all, and I translated for each. Walker seemed to be particularly eager to encounter the enemy. He understood that by success as a soldier only could he claim consideration in the country. Castelloñ, who felt himself about equally exposed to destruction from the hostile acts of the enemy in arms against his government and the machinations of General Muñoz, commanding his own army, seemed glad of the interposition of the foreigner, whose strength was not to be gauged by his present number of adherents, but referred to future possibilities.

General Muñoz, who came in during the interview, presented both in his nature and appearance a striking contrast to Colonel Walker. Between the two as marked an antipathy was observable as that exhibited in the sudden encounter between a dog and a cat. Walker's manner was short and abrupt, while his appearance was of the plainest. Muñoz, on the contrary, was a man of the most striking physical beauty, wore the handsome uniform of a Major-General, and was a master of those graces of manner which often influence our judgments of character.

Muñoz affected to treat the matter of the American alliance as unimportant in national affairs, and nothing was effected in the interview. Later, the President promised Walker that as soon as Muñoz departed on an expedition then ready to march for the purpose of checking the depredations of the enemy on the rich cattle estates of the province of Segovia, a native auxiliary force should be furnished to Col. Walker to aid him in recovering from the enemy the transit route which they had seized as soon as the Democrats evacuated Granada.

Walker's object in making the transit route the theatre of his operations was twofold. It gave him a command independent and separate from General Muñoz. If he could establish and maintain a footing on that line, he could communicate with available reinforcements congregated in California.

The necessary authority for this separate expedition having at length been obtained from the Minister of war, who also directed Colonel Ramirez to report to Walker with two

The "Filibuster" War in Nicaragua. 111

hundred native infantry, the expeditionary force prepared to embark at Realejo for the purpose of capturing the transit route from the enemy. Our reasonable expectation was that the Democrats of the meridional department would flock to our standard as soon as we could offer them guaranties of protection.

The little band of men whom Walker had brought with him was admirably officered. I had been active in promoting the arrangement by which Colonel Walker would have an opportunity to test his ability to conquer a peace from the enemy, free from interference of the intriguing commander-in-chief, but hardly saw how I could associate myself with their completed organization.

Hitherto my position, though restricted in power, had been singularly independent, and I was averse from accepting the position of aide to the commanding officer. He was wholly unacquainted with the people and their mode of warfare, but during my short acquaintance with him he had developed an amount of wilfulness in small things which augured a despotic character, which I was unwilling to subject myself to. When, however, I announced my intention of remaining at Leon, I found that not only

Colonel Walker, but his officers had counted so much on my accompanying them that, sacrificing my better judgment to the feeling of regard for my countrymen, to whom I well knew that my acquired experience would be valuable, I consented to accompany them. Mendez declared that if I went he, too, would go, which he did, prompted, no doubt, by the love of adventurous strife, which had become to him as the breath of his nostrils. Walker, who seemed to comprehend the character of this soldier of fortune, remarked to me in English, as soon as Mendez had concluded his expressions of devotion to the Americans, and to the "sacred cause of liberty," that he had no doubt Mendez' exchequer had run low, and he expected to replenish it at the expense of the enemy.

The force was embarked in the brig Vesta, and left the harbor of Realejo on the 23d of June, 1855.

Colonel Ramirez, whom I had known in the service at Granada, a morose and inconspicuous officer, had been tardy in reporting his command to Colonel Walker. Instead of the five hundred promised, it consisted of less than a hundred and fifty. Certain of my Nicaraguan friends had cautioned me that he was not only a man of inferior capacity and courage in the field, but was also a tool of Muñoz. Walker, to whom I imparted this information, seemed to care but little about it. The reason for his indifference was his inordinate confidence in the ability of his handful of Americans to conquer, unassisted, any number of the enemy. His errors of judgment, on which I shall have occasion again to comment, were the faults of a very brave man, but none the less faults, as they involved miscalculations in the adaptation of means to an end, besides occasioning frequent and useless loss of life.

> " Our remedies oft in ourselves do lie
> Which we ascribe to heaven."

After four miserable days, tossed hither and thither by contrary winds, we reached a small harbor a few leagues above San Juan del Sur, at *El Gigante*, near Brito, the harbor, by-the-bye, destined at some future day, when the interests of commerce are able to command the attention of legislators unbiassed by private interests, to be the terminus of an interoceanic canal, as it is by far the most feasible route that has been proposed.

I speak advisedly on this point, having had

opportunities personally to compare the different routes proposed.

This point was chosen by Walker for a landing, because he very naturally looked for the enemy, who doubtless were well informed of the departure of the expedition from Realejo, to attempt a strong opposition to our landing at San Juan.

And as he contemplated attacking them in their stronghold at Rivas, the present landing was equally favorable for that purpose, and less likely to subject him to annoyance on the march thither.

I had been exceedingly ill during the voyage from an attack of dysentery, and suffered besides from sea-sickness, so the doctor recommended me not to land, for, even under favorable conditions for transportation, I was unfit for duty. The conditions were most unfavorable, for the march of twenty miles to Rivas must be in darkness and drenching rain over trackless hills.

But no argument short of a clear presentation of the impossibility of my getting through would have deterred me from making the attempt, and the Colonel promised that I should have such aid as could be given by the soldiers.

In landing, the boat in which I was was permitted to strike the ground, and such was my weakness, that the shock threw me overboard. But for the active exertions of the men, I should doubtless have been drowned.

We began the march about midnight in a heavy down-pour of rain. To add to our difficulties the trail was hard to find in the darkness, so that we had to wait in the heavy rain for the partial clearing of the sky. It would be hard to imagine a more miserable object than I felt myself to be as I lay down on the bare sodden ground. When the trail was found, we resumed the march. A soldier supported me on each side, for I was too weak to stand by myself.

The following day the rain abated, but the walking was fearfully bad. It was not until about nine o'clock at night that we came to the small village of Tola. Then it was raining again harder than I ever saw it. We were now within about nine miles of Rivas, though in no condition to attack that place, so we were fain to content ourselves with the near prospect of rest and shelter in the village. Some of our natives, who knew the locality, informed us that there was a government *quartel* in the place, at which it was customary to keep a picket in time of war as a protection and means of information to the army in Rivas.

As we marched along the single street looking for the *quartel*—the heavy down-pour of rain completely deadening the sound of our footsteps,—we came suddenly to the quarters of the soldiers, in the corridor of which were two or three groups playing cards by the light of tallow dips, the sentinel having withdrawn under the porch to escape the rain. His quick challenge of "Quien vive!" was followed as he perceived us by the discharge of his musket, and the Americans, who were in advance of our native troops, rushed upon the building without waiting for orders, shooting and overpowering all opposition in a few moments.

Several of the enemy were killed and wounded, without loss on our part, and we soon disposed our native troops to guard the place, while the Americans sought rest; well knowing that on the following day they would need all their surplus energy. For myself I was indisposed to sleep, probably because of reaction from the stupor induced by the drugs which the doctor had given me.

CHAPTER VIII.

Battle of Rivas—Retreat to San Juan.

THE heavy rain of the night was followed in the morning by a glorious sunshine, in the warm rays of which the soldiers dried their clothing and arms. Beef and chickens were plenty, and a satisfactory breakfast was soon prepared. We were only about nine miles from Rivas. Our exploit of the previous night had well warned the enemy of our approach, so there was no need for either secrecy or hurry on our part.

Information from various sources apprised us that Colonel Bosque, the Commandant at Rivas, had been advised of our approach as soon after our debarkation as fast runners could carry the news; further, that, as he had been for weeks barricading and fortifying the town, and would, besides, rely on aid from the citizens and a military force of twelve hundred picked men, the presumption was that we need not long spoil for want of a fight. It was evident from the bearing of our men, their eagerness, and elaborate preparations of their arms, that a fight was exactly what would suit them, and what they had come for. Weary as I had become of the long and inconsequent struggle at Granada and the apparently useless sacrifice of life, I was not without hope for a better issue for the war, now that men of energy and determination were in command. We had now probably to attack from five to ten times our numbers—that would depend on the backing of the towns-people,—but I saw no need for despairing of success, provided our native auxiliaries should efficiently second the Americans, and that Colonel Walker should prove the sagacious leader which his men had declared him to be.

We resumed the march to Rivas about nine A. M., proceeding in a leisurely way, that indicated confidence as well as determination.

Many market women were met returning with their empty baskets, and as discipline was relaxed, owing to our feeling sure that the enemy would keep on the other side of their barricades, the men were permitted to chaff and question the women as they pleased, who were not reluctant to interchange civilities. I noticed that while Walker and the American officers seemed indifferent to the acquisition of information relating to the numbers and disposition of the enemy, Colonel Ramirez made particular inquiries on these points; the full significance of this was revealed by subsequent events. Two hours' march brought us to the environs of the town, and we had no sooner reached the paved streets than we came upon a barricade, through which protruded the muzzle of a twenty-four pounder, a protest not to be disregarded. It now became necessary to adopt some method of attack. Colonel Walker ordered the men to form two abreast, and then instructed Tejada to direct Colonel Ramirez to follow the Americans until the latter were fairly in the town. Then Ramirez was to distribute his men at those outlets of the San Juan and Granada roads by which the enemy might attempt to escape, leaving us to deal with the force in the plaza.

Tejada, sometimes known as Napoleon, was so confounded by the order, that he could not translate it to Ramirez. He begged the Colonel to repeat it, which he having done, poor Tejada, though perfectly comprehending the words, hesitated about communicating them, until Walker exasperated, sent him to the rear, and requested me to convey his order. This I did at once; the eyes of Ramirez sparkled as he perceived how favorable the disposition was for furthering his ulterior views. I was as astonished as Tejada. I had been fighting these men for a year now, and knew that success against such fearful odds could only be attained by indomitable courage, combined with judicious stratagem. Walker's experience in fighting the Spanish-Americans had been confined to the sage-brush nurtured inhabitants of Sonora, who were ready to fly at the sound of their own guns. He was evidently committing the grave error in a commanding officer, of undervaluing his enemy. I therefore, while the orders were being executed, trusted to my long experience and my independent position as volunteer aide, and suggested to Colonel Walker that it would be better not to send our native troops out of our reach, until we saw what need we might have for them as supports in our attack.

With the smile which we afterwards learned to understand the meaning of so well, he replied that I had not yet seen what fifty-six such men as he had, and so armed, could do; and feeling that, owing to our limited acquaintance, further remonstrance from me might be misinterpreted,

I merely bowed as I took my place at his side. For the first time I lost faith in our success, but determined that no duty or effort of mine should be neglected on that account.

As soon as our little column came within range of the twenty-four pounder, we charged impetuously, and were saluted with a discharge of grape and canister, which, owing to the suddenness of our forward movement, nearly all passed over our heads, while Ramirez, who probably foresaw the greater danger of following in our immediate rear, did not move his men until we had cleared the way. We quickly scaled the barricade, only to find a similar one a little farther on, behind which those who had manned the first were struggling to obtain a shelter from our pursuit. Without wasting time in firing at these fellows, we kept on after them, reaching the second barricade without having sustained much damage. We were here met by a pretty steady firing from the loop-holed walls in the cross streets, which we could not return with much effect, and therefore kept on towards the plaza.

As we neared this base of the enemy's operations, their converging fire from the sides and front of the broad street became very heavy, and to avoid in part the storm of bullets that hurtled through the air around us, we kept close to the houses on either side. Our chief difficulty thus far had been that, while exposed to the enemy's fire, they were nearly invisible to us, sheltered behind their loop-holed walls.

We were now near enough to their stronghold to feel a cross-fire that, with better aim, should have annihilated us, and we also found that the more substantial nature of their defences made further progress impossible, except by the slow and laborious method of picks and crowbars. There were so few of us that we had not carried sapping and mining implements, hence there was nothing for us but to keep up a kind of scattering fire at the loop-holes, wherever a head or musket offered a mark. The aim of our men was true enough to make even this fire very destructive, but the odds of number and position were fearfully against us. Already we were counting our dead and wounded. Emboldened by our enforced halt, they had made several attempts at charging us, but had been promptly and fiercely repulsed. At length our men began to show signs of unwillingness to be made the target for an overwhelming force, whom they could not get at, and refused to continue an assault on solid wall. Major Crocker, at this juncture, approached Walker, one arm which had been broken by a bullet dangling by his side, and announced that the men could not be brought to charge the enemy, who were pressing them from an alley in the rear.

In all former experiences I had been more or less a commander. Here, and especially after the repulse which my suggestion of keeping the native force near us had met with, I had only executed orders, and, as I carried my trusty rifle, had acted on the general principle of " firing wherever I could see a head." Walker now turned to me and asked if I could make any suggestion for our extrication from the immediate surroundings. After our passage of the first barricade, we had seen no more of our native auxiliaries, and I was satisfied that Ramirez did not intend to support us ; he had ample excuse for defection in Colonel Walker's injudicious order. As soon as it had been fairly demonstrated that we could not get at the enemy, my tactics—learned by experience in this kind of warfare—would have been instantly to withdraw my men from under fire, and seek a junction with our native forces preparatory to attack on some more accessible point. At this late hour it was doubtful whether an attempt at withdrawal would not prove suicidal. I was, however, spared decision by Walker's suggestion that a temporary shelter and rest would put the men in condition to resume offensive operations in the direction of the plaza. I therefore pointed to a large and very solid building on the opposite side of the street, and recommended that the front folding-doors should be battered down, and we take possession of it as a temporary fortress.

This was instantly done; we found ourselves for the moment sheltered from the rain of missiles, and the men set about making the best arrangements for defence possible in such a place. Foreseeing that our abandoning the offensive would stimulate the enemy to assume that rôle, I urged resolution and unity, and set an example of activity by throwing a heavy piece of furniture in front of the wide open doorway. In this I was quickly seconded by Colonel Walker and Lieut.-Col. Kewen, and none too soon, for we had scarcely opposed a temporary barrier, when a well-organized assault with fixed bayonets was made by the enemy. Had they got in on us in these close quarters, where rifles were useless, with their large numbers they would have quickly made an end of us. As it was, the temporary barrier enabled the men to recover from the momentary lethargy which seemed to have seized them, and while Kewen, Walker, and myself actually beat them back, turning aside their bayonets and thrusting at them with our swords, the men came up, and firing over our shoulders, soon checked the advance and heaped the door-way with the bodies of our enemies. They first paused, and then hastily withdrew, leaving a hecatomb of their dead as witness of the unerring aim of the rifles.

As the fire of our men released us from the pressure of the enemy, Colonel Kewen staggered forward, clutching the air with his hands. I caught him and laid him gently on his back. There was no need to ask how badly he was hurt, for the purple stream issuing from his lips, and a red spot in the centre of his breast from which too the blood flowed rapidly, told the story. He had been shot through the lung, and smilingly sank in death.

The severity of the enemy's loss taught them more caution, but did not seem to lessen their energies. They pressed into the streets, swarming around and even setting fire to the canes and light material that supported the tiles over our heads. Every moment seemed to draw the net of doom closer about us. Some quick action was imperative.

The men seemed to have lost their early energy and courage. Walker, since we had abandoned the offensive, seemed also to have been stricken with the general torpor, and I, by a kind of spontaneous action, had for the time assumed command.

I encouraged the men by taking their loaded rifles and firing them through the open door-way at the masses of the enemy who occupied the street. The bullets, enfilading this opening, and the windows as well, might have taught me that by such exposure I courted death, but since that threatened any way, I could afford indifference to the time and manner of its coming. A ball struck me in the right temple, and I dropped to the floor. I remember a flickering sensation as of a struggle to keep down to the earth in opposition to a gravitative impulse upward, and then I distinctly heard Captain Hornsby say, "He's gone," and Colonel Walker reply, "It is a pity." The words, or else the profuse flow of the blood, relieved the temporary confusion caused by the blow, and springing to my feet I shouted that I was "not gone yet," the words eliciting a cheer amid even our sad surroundings.

I asked for the surgeon, for the bullet, cutting the temporal artery, caused great waste of blood. He assured me, however, from his perch near the rafters, that it would soon stop of itself.

At this time the tiled floor of the large room in which we were assembled was strewn with the dead bodies of our comrades, the sight of whose ghastly visages seemed to paralyze the nerves of many of the men. Colonel Kewen, Major Crocker, and many brave men were dead; many others were more or less severely wounded.

The enemy were bringing a heavy gun to bear upon the building. A wall which they were demolishing was the only obstacle at present intervening between us. In this crisis Walker and Hornsby came to me, the former asking if I could suggest any way for temporary relief, adding that he hoped that when night should fall we might still be able to make a successful assault on the plaza. Our fortress was but a short distance from a kind of moat or ravine bordered by trees, and although the intervening space was crowded by the enemy, I told the Colonel that I thought our only chance of escape was to make a dash, when, if successful in forcing a passage, fighting along the top of the moat would be easier than in the streets.

The suggestion was received with a shout, and we at once formed, to put it in execution.

The men, seeing that a supreme effort was to be made, recovered their vigor, and our charge was made with such impetuosity that we were firing our revolvers in our opponents' faces and thrusting our way through their ranks before they had any notion of what we were about. Colonel Walker and myself, after forming the line, had taken our places at the head of the column for the assault, when poor " Hughes," about the last remaining of my riflemen in the Jalteva, called to me from a corner of the room where he lay wounded, begging me not to leave him.

These are the emergencies harder to meet than any in the mere strife of battle.

Any hesitation at this moment would have been fatal to all, besides being useless to him.

Before the enemy could disengage themselves from us we had passed through their midst, and, turning as we reached the sloping bank of the ravine, were ready to give them a warm reception if they desired to follow us. This did not for the moment seem to be their plan, so we deliberately began retiring along the edge of the ravine, and in a short time found ourselves in the open country outside the town. We continued our way slowly, fully expecting to be pursued and attacked by the foe, whom we felt competent to cope with as soon as we were clear of the buildings, which sheltered them from the aim of the riflemen. They did not follow us, and we halted near the village of San Jorge, in order to form some plans and to redistribute the ammunition.

While thus engaged, the bells in the churches at Rivas rang out a peal of victory.

It had cost them dearly, however, for their dead alone doubled in number the handful of men whom they, twenty to one, had contended against. At this place, Captain Mayorga and two or three others, who, like Mendez, had voluntarily joined the expedition, came to us from the adjoining thicket, and from them we learned that, at the beginning of the engagement, Colonel Ramirez had marched his troops straight away from the town, and taken the road to the neighboring state of Costa Rica. Colonel Walker subsequently made a charge to

President Castelloñ against General Muñoz, accusing him of having given secret instructions to Ramirez, who was known as his tool, to desert the Americans in this manner as soon as they were fairly within the enemy's lines.

I have no doubt of Ramirez' treason, but, had Walker shown more regard for, and reliance on, our native troops, by keeping them with us to share in the battle, there was enough of loyalty among them, as well as of hatred for the enemy, to have assured us their support. I have always found the common soldier among the Central Americans, as elsewhere, freer from the vice of treachery than their leaders, treason being a crime more common to a higher class.

The last that I had seen of Mendez was when we took shelter in the building. He was replacing the red ribbon which he tore from his hat by a white handkerchief, and Captain Mayorga informed us that he had seized a riderless horse and ridden boldly through the streets, saved by the white badge on his hat. It was just like Mendez, and I was glad to learn of his escape.

Colonel Walker decided to march towards San Juan del Sur, and, as Mayorga was a native of Rivas, and well acquainted with the country, he was directed to guide us through bye-ways to the San Juan road.

So profound, however, was Walker's distrust of the native character since the treachery of Ramirez, that he requested me to inform Captain Mayorga that if he should lead us into an ambush, his life would pay the forfeit, since every man had orders, in that event, to shoot him.

In vain Mayorga, who was doubtless quite loyal to us, pleaded that the enemy might lie in wait for us among the thickets we had to pass through. Walker was inexorable, and we resumed our way through thickets and briars under his guidance. Colonel Walker and myself kept close to the guide with cocked revolvers, a precaution against his running away, as well as a guard against his possible treachery.

Walker now became as anxious to reach the sea-shore ahead of the enemy as before he had been indifferent to their movements. Out of consideration for the wounded, among whom were Lieutenant—afterward Colonel—Anderson, and Captain Du Brissott, I had told the guide not to hurry, but soon Walker ordered me to direct Captain Hornsby to increase the pace of the men. He added quietly that the wounded must take their chances, since our only hope of escape from the enemy depended upon our getting possession of San Juan with the sea at our backs before they anticipated us. I thought of my advice of the morning, which he had treated rather contemptuously, but none the less I made up my mind that, if I could help it, the wounded should not be left behind. After directing me two or three times to increase the speed of the march, I think he suspected that I was delaying it, and himself gave the order to go faster. But the wounded men had by this time been provided with horses.

Through darkness and Mayorga's fright, we became entangled in the thickets. At midnight, when about exhausted, we came to a small cattle ranch, and there a halt was called for the night.

Walker, partly from resentment for the defection of Ramirez, partly as a precautionary measure, caused the old ranchero and his wife to be guarded as hostages for the fealty of their sons. These were directed to slaughter and prepare for the men's breakfast an ox from the corral. They were warned that their parents' safety and payment for the ox depended on their faith, for they could easily apprise the army at Rivas of our condition.

Colonel Walker and myself, alone of the tired

company, tried to keep watch over the camp, and I soon saw my commander yielding to the influence of sleep.

I suppose the effects of my sickness and subsequent exertions, together with the loss of blood from my wound, helped to keep me awake, for I had no inclination to sleep, although this was my third night of wakefulness. An extreme nervous tension seemed to have taken the place of a more healthful drowsiness. I sat the long night through, occasionally chatting with the old farmer and his wife, the latter of whom seemed anxious to know whether we would not kill them before leaving in the morning, and was much comforted, though surprised, at my assurance that the Americans never killed prisoners. In the morning, while the men were getting their breakfasts, Surgeon Jones extracted the ounce ball from my skull, near the ear, using a jack-knife and his fingers, in place of the instruments he had thrown away in exchange for a rifle, in our extremity at Rivas.

As he sharpened the blade on a pebble preparatory to the operation, I cautioned him that a very little pressure of the dull instrument would push the bullet through the fractured bone, but he managed the operation skilfully.

The march was resumed after a good breakfast, and the unwounded men seemed able to do good service against any enemy in the path.

We were soon in sight of the transit road, about at the half-way house, six miles from San Juan. The fatiguing march of many miles had been through the dense and thorny thickets, and since I, at the head of the column, had helped to break the road, my thin boots had been actually torn from my feet, which left bleeding traces as I walked.

The prospect of the even gravel of the road was pleasant to some; so was the assurance it gave of an approaching ending to the march.

To me the miles ahead were as formidable as if the distance were interminable, for I felt that my strength was at last giving out, and that I could not much longer keep up with the march.

As the men, with renewed alacrity, prepared to push through the remaining bushes to the road, the footfalls of an approaching cavalcade resounded in the near distance.

Walker, with the promptness that distinguished him in emergencies, ordered every man to conceal himself, and on no account to fire unless he gave the word.

Immediately afterwards a body of cavalry

wearing the hated white ribbon, came along four abreast. In the centre of their column was the gayly caparisoned mule team of the express company, the treasure of which they were escorting.

A single well-directed volley, such as the Americans were capable of delivering at the short range at which we were, would have emptied as many saddles as there were rifles among us, and we should have replaced the escort over the treasure. The forbearance of Walker, when his enemy was at his mercy, in the interests of property and the moral force which attends its protection, should sharply rebuke the insensate cry of "Filibuster" that subsequently attached to his name.

For myself, who have known him so well, the act has no significance; it was only an instance of his usual regard for and observance of justice where no great public stake was involved.

The soldiers passed harmlessly over that very pit of Avernus, which would have yawned for them at a single word from one man, and we resumed our march. Stimulated by an even road and the proximity of a port in which some vessel was sure to be found to carry the handful of worn-out men away from their legion of enemies, the movement quickened so much, that, as I gradually dropped to the rear, I saw myself in imagination left to solitude on a road infested by enemies. As I have seen horses after a long march in the desert hasten forward when the moisture-laden air betokens water near by, so every uninjured man now pressed onward, heedless of those less strong than themselves, Wearily dragging myself along, I perceived a single horseman approaching from the front, and what was more remarkable, he kept on his way, though the red ribbons of our party, as well as their nationality and consequent political affinity, were easily discernible at that distance. As it was unsafe for any one to declare himself a Democrat in this locality, at the present time, the conduct of the solitary horseman implied boldness and democracy combined. He was soon seen to be an American, and as he came up, the column was halted for Colonel Walker to obtain information about the condition of the road ahead and about the force of the enemy in San Juan.

The man proved to be a Mr. Dewey, a Kentuckian, and former member of my rifle company at Granada. Dewey, who was a noted desperado and California gambler, had nevertheless been a good soldier at the Jalteva, and had been discharged at his request when I formed a native company. He had since that time thriven in his profession at San Juan. He now announced that the news of our being in the woods, after the unsuccessful attempt at the capture of Rivas, had been brought to San Juan, and that he had come out hoping to meet us, and to tell us that there were no troops either in San Juan, or, as far as he knew, in the neighborhood.

CHAPTER IX.

Seizure of a Costa Rican brig—Burning of the barracks—Escape from San Juan—Death of Dewey—Dangerous navigation—In a fishing-smack—On the sick-list—Preparations for another expedition.

FROM my knowledge of Dewey's character, I was able to assure Colonel Walker that no treachery was to be feared from him where the lives of his countrymen were involved.

Strange anomaly in human nature! The man burdened with crime and violence, a hunted fugitive from the law's decrees, is still the inheritor of honorable instincts that cause him to risk his life for his countrymen, when self-interest would prompt him to seek alliance with the dominant party.

The safety of the road and town being thus assured, the command pressed forward with increased speed, and I was quickly left behind, every one being too much absorbed in the chance of making an escape by sea before the arrival of a large force of the enemy from Rivas, to care for those less able than themselves to get along,

Such was my weakness from exhaustion, and the intense pain caused by contact of the hard gravel with my lacerated feet, that I abandoned all hope or care to keep up with the rest, and was looking for a resting-place by the wayside, when Dewey, looking back and perceiving my plight, rode back, and helping me up behind his saddle, rescued me from the inevitable fate which awaited those who from wounds or exhaustion were left behind. I am glad to record the good act of this man, who subsequently paid with his life the penalty of many crimes.

The sight of San Juan and the blue Pacific Ocean was most welcome to the shattered and exhausted remnant, and still more hopeful was the suggestion raised by the sight of a handsome schooner just anchoring in the port. Captain Hornsby, with a detail of men, was quickly aboard of her. She proved to be the San Jose, of Costa Rica, and was held by him under military necessity as a means for our escape from the numerous enemy. Hornsby arrived none too soon, for the Dutch captain and trader, seeing the American soldiers on shore, and surmising the situation, was already weighing his anchor preparatory to getting away from such unprofitable customers. Nothing was to be gained by delay, and it was important to get aboard before the arrival of the enemy from Rivas, so no time was lost in embarking the men. I was taken on board with the rest of the wounded at once, and carried to the cabin. There I found instant relief from suffering and exhaustion, in a sleep so profound that many of the exciting events that followed, some of them close to my berth, were only known to me as they were subsequently recounted by the various actors therein.

Night was closing in as the last of the men, excepting the small picket, were put on board, and, as its shadows were darkening the landscape, a lurid glow shot up from the barracks near the beach. The whole structure was soon ablaze. Dewey, and a sailor named Sam, the owner of a fishing-smack, had fired the building, in the mere wantonness and malice of men who sought to inflict damage on a place, the inhabitants of which were getting tired of harboring them and permitting the exercise of their nefarious pursuits. As it was intended, the odium fell on the Americans, under the ægis of whose power the act was committed, Walker was very much incensed, and determined to mete that justice to the perpetrators which should herald to the world that, however his ambition might seek power through legitimate means, no mere vandalism could receive his sanction.

Sam, in a semi-drunken condition, came aboard to seek favor for what he regarded as a meritorious act. He was seized, and, pending ebb-tide, needed to get away from the dangerous shore, since there was no wind, he was tried by a hastily summoned court-martial, sitting in the cabin close to where I slept, and, in a few minutes, convicted and condemned to be shot, Walker approving the sentence.

Captain Hornsby, with a detail to carry the sentence into execution, conveyed the prisoner ashore. There, in the darkness, and amid the confusion attendant upon the approach and scattering fire from the advanced guard of the enemy, who had thus tardily arrived from Rivas, he managed to slip the hempen shackles which bound his wrists, and to escape.

I have always doubted whether some sympathizing soldier did not aid him in loosening his bonds, a thing easily done under cover of night.

Dewey, though drunk, had been too wise to trust himself on board, and had taken refuge on the smack, expecting that Sam would shortly arrive and cast loose the vessel from the locality already made dangerous to them by the arrival of the enemy. As the baffled detail came aboard, amid the scattering fire of the enemy, who were forming on the beach, they towed the smack to the schooner, to which they made her fast, and the tide having begun to ebb, we slowly left the port for the open sea. A little more enterprise on the part of the enemy would have made it impossible for us to get away. Perhaps their supineness is not to be wondered at, considering the great loss they had sustained the day before, and their probable belief that the Americans would never again return to hazard a similarly warm welcome.

It was not until we arrived at Leon that we heard of the fate of the half-dozen wounded men whom we had left in Rivas.

They were chained upon a pile of faggots collected in the plaza and burned alive, by order of the commandant, Colonel Bosque, on the evening of the day of the battle, an expiatory sacrifice to the manes of those who had fallen at our hands. Colonel Walker, in giving an account of this, his first battle in Nicaragua, is careful to underestimate his loss and the size of the force he persisted in contending against, when a wiser judgment, not implying less courage, would have caused him to withdraw from the net prepared for him as soon as he had seen the hopelessness of persistence. Experience is a valuable teacher, though we may not be always willing to acknowledge our obligations to her. Though our force was small in number, it is seldom that the annals of history have to chronicle an effort of more hardihood and daring than that of this little band, deserted, as they were in the beginning by their allies. It is certain that one-third of them were killed or rendered *hors de combat* by wounds.

I was awakened the next morning by Walker himself, who said he wished me to speak to the native woman (Sam's mistress), who was steering the smack in tow of the schooner. As I reached the deck, much refreshed by the night's sleep, though suffering from the pain of my wound, the blood from which stiffened my clothing, I found the schooner bounding along before a stiff breeze, the sunlight sparkling on the crested billows, and the mountains of the Nicaraguan coast close a-starboard. The little smack was tugging at the line which fastened her to our taffrail, her tiller tightly grasped in the nut-brown hands of the comely woman who passed as Mrs. Sam. Two riflemen were stationed at the taffrail of the schooner with orders to shoot Dewey if he should make any attempt to cast loose the line which held the smack in tow, and, as he was known to be a desperado who would never yield while he could fight, it was desirable to get the woman aboard the schooner, out of the way of bullets. I was therefore directed to ask her in Spanish to come forward, so that we could assist her on board. This she promptly attempted, but was forbidden by Dewey, who, first placing two large navy revolvers on the hatch, slowly followed, and stepping on the deck of the little vessel, demanded to know what we wanted.

I called to him that Colonel Walker demanded that he should come aboard the schooner and stand his trial for burning the government barracks at San Juan.

He answered that Colonel Walker might go to hell. At the same time he stepped forward to cast the towing line off.

"Don't do that, Dewey," I called to him. "The men have orders to shoot you if you attempt it." His answer was to stoop down and grasp a navy revolver in each hand. As he proceeded to cock them, two shots rang out from the sentinels at my side, and Dewey pitched forward beneath the hatch.

At the same moment the woman at the tiller shrieked that she was shot.

I directed her to come forward, whence she was helped aboard the schooner.

The surgeon found that one of the rifle-balls after piercing Dewey's body had entered her thigh, causing a dangerous wound, which she recovered from only after a long and painful illness.

As the men who fired the shots had been selected marksmen, there was no need to enquire about the fate of Dewey, and, as Walker no longer needed my services on board, he, with an admirable sense of utility, and regardless of my wounded condition, requested me to go on board, take charge of the smack, and bring her into Realejo. He constituted me on the spot administrator of Sam's effects, and detailed two soldiers to accompany me to work the vessel over the hundred and odd miles of ocean intervening between us and Realejo.

It was always a part of my military creed to hear and to obey, and I did not think of interposing any objection on account of my weakened condition and undressed wound, but followed the two men over the side as best I could. The line was cast off, the schooner sped away with increased velocity, and we were left pitching about on the sea.

The men had gone down the hatchway, and, as I took the tiller of the boat, I called to them to come up and hoist the sail, for after casting loose from the schooner, we were rolling in the troughs of the sea.

When they came on deck some little time afterwards, they reported Dewey quite dead, shot through the heart.

I learned afterwards that these men rushed into the hold as soon as they got aboard, in order to search the clothing of the gambler, who was reputed to have a considerable sum in gold about him, and that they did in fact find a prize. When, after having set the sail, I ordered them to lift the body on deck preparatory to its burial in the sea, and requested them to search it for valuables, it is certain that they declared they found none.

They were men of a worse stamp than Dewey himself. One of them subsequently killed a comrade in a manner impossible to justify in any way, for which deed he would have been shot by a sentence of court-martial, had he not happened to have been a useful soldier at a time when every man counted. The sense of justice was subordinated to that of utility.

I soon found that I was in no enviable position on the wide sea with these men, who, when I told them to sew the body of Dewey in a sail and put shot at the feet, replied that there was no use taking that trouble, it being easier to toss it over as it was. I was very weak, and should have been utterly unable to cope with either of these ruffians in a contest of strength, but as they knew nothing of the coast or of navigation, I had some power over them, and ordered them to do as I had bid them.

It was the least I could do for the man who, whatever his crimes, had performed a disinterested act of kindness that had probably saved my life. When the sack containing his body cleft the blue water, I only remembered the brave man, forgetting for the moment that the Nemesis which pursued him to the death was but the just retribution for some of the acts of his life. Alas! which of us can afford to throw the first stone? And are we not after all subject to the law of necessity, like the two small tiger cubs which Sam had in the hold as pets, who, as soon as Dewey fell helpless under the fatal bullets, tore his breast in obedience to ferocious natural instinct?

When every thing was placed in orderly condition on the little craft, finding the sea too high for comfort if not for safety, I steered nearer the shore than strict prudence warranted, hoping to avail ourselves of the smoother water near the mountainous coast, from whence the wind blew. I was congratulating myself on the relief from the tossing waters, when the sail flapping against the mast warned us that we were under the lee of the mountains, and becalmed.

With neither oar nor sweep aboard, we were entirely at the mercy of the currents and undertow.

Night fell around us in this condition, and as we had neither glass nor compass, we could only drift aimlessly about, the greater blackness of the sky near the shore alone notifying us of its proximity.

Towards morning, the gradually increasing sound of breakers indicated that we were drifting shoreward, but as we had no means of counteracting the currents that were carrying us in, having neither sweep nor oar, we were obliged philosophically to await the impending end. As soon as the boat should be caught in the breakers, whose white, dashing spray was already visible through the darkness, only a strong swimmer might hope to save himself.

The men stripped themselves for the struggle, and I, who had neither strength nor inclination for the necessary effort, reclined by the tiller with a sense of relief that the incessant struggle of life would soon be over.

During these waiting moments, in which we seemed to be slowly forging onward to destruction, I suddenly felt a puff of wind on my face. Calling to the men to brace the yard sharp, I had the satisfaction to see the sail draw tight, and the boat, answering to the helm, we sheered slowly but steadily away from the dreadful breakers, whose thunderous sound filled the air. We had probably been passing a cleft or cañon in the mountains, through which the wind found escape from the otherwise impassable barrier to the sea, and by keeping the boat well before it, we regained the rough water, and had the wind from over the tops of the mountains.

The next day and night we kept on, with more moderate wind and smoother water. Inflammation had set in from my wound, and I suffered a good deal, but more troublesome than any physical pain was the conduct of the men, who urged that it were better to set up as free rovers in a good craft than, by rejoining the desperate fortunes of Colonel Walker in a land and cause beset by enemies, inevitably meet with hardship and death.

Our vessel, they argued, would hold a dozen bold men, whom we could without difficulty pick up in the small seaports, and then we could levy contributions wherever we chose in the sparsely settled hamlets along the coast.

They were in earnest, and but for their lack of confidence in their ability to lead themselves, would doubtless have thrown me overboard. The sight, on our third day upon the sea, of the tall masts of the Vesta, through an opening in the rock-bound coast we were passing, was most welcome to me.

Soon after casting loose from us, the people on the "San Jose" had descried the Vesta cruising near "El Gigante," and, being a very rapid sailor, gave chase. The Vesta, taking her for an enemy, since she flew the Costa Rican flag, tried to get away, but was overhauled, and the men were transferred aboard her.

She was now in the harbor at Realejo, and

we were soon lying alongside her. Having resigned my charge to Captain Morton, I proceeded in a row-boat to the town, where, fortunately for me, I found my friend Dr. Dawson, of Chinendega.

From the effects of my wound and exposure, fever had already set in, and the good doctor had me conveyed in a cart to his home in Chinendega, where for weeks he and his excellent Spanish wife gave me that care which, with my excellent constitution, effected a cure.

During my sickness and convalescence the "American phalanx," as it was called, remained in Realejo and Chinendega.

The renown which they obtained by their former expedition to Rivas, although resulting in defeat, was such that great expectations were attached to them. Their losses were more than made good by the accession to their ranks of stray Americans, attracted by their popularity, and they were indeed more formidable, thanks to the experience they had gained, than before.

The conduct of Ramirez and his men was keenly felt and regretted by the more sensitive of the Democratic leaders, prominent among whom was General *Valle*, commonly called Chelon. He was an especial pet of the soldiers of the Chinendega department, where he commanded, and who, besides entertaining an intense dislike for Muñoz, secretly aspired to the dictatorship of the country, for which position his popularity and fighting proclivities rendered him peculiarly fitted. Besides this, he was a man of very generous impulses, and his present wish, as he said, was to show the Americans that all Central Americans were neither traitors nor cowards.

When Walker failed to obtain official aid from the Leon government, owing to the factions which opposed the President, and marched his force to Realejo, with the threat of seeking in Honduras, whither the President had cordially invited him, that employment for his arms which faction denied him in Nicaragua, Chelon, who had but to say to his soldiers "Come on," and they would follow him against their President himself, if required, declared that he would accompany Walker again to the Transit route with an adequate force to wipe out the stain of Ramirez' treason from the people of Nicaragua.

This was after all the easiest solution of the question for the President, and active preparations soon resulted in placing on the brig

Vesta and a ketch as consort about one hundred and fifty native soldiers with Chelon at their head,—a force in every sense reliable, making with the Americans a little army sure to give a good account of themselves hereafter.

After I had again been able to report for duty, my time was mostly employed in making such preparations as, in my capacity of commissary and quartermaster, would put the Americans again on a war footing, having ample authority to give vouchers in the name of the government for necessary supplies. The government's credit was good, so I had little difficulty in obtaining what the country could provide.

There was one exception to this rule.

A Mr. Manning, formerly British Consul at Chinendega, who had become wealthy on the monopolies which the power of his government had enabled him to procure from the Church government in Nicaragua, chanced to have the only supply of rifle-powder and percussion caps in the town. They were a part of his merchandise, and I sent a sergeant with the necessary government vouchers for their purchase. He refused to sell them, using language disrespectful to the Democratic government and boasting of the protection he derived from that of Great Britain. I consulted Colonel Walker, for I wished to be cautious in giving cause for quarrel against the government.

Walker said that as munitions of war they were to be seized, provided Manning would not sell them. I therefore took a file of men, and as Manning, when I approached his door, placed the ensign of St. George across it, making dire threats of British vengeance if I should molest it, I quietly, but with proper respect for the emblem of a great nation, placed it on one side and took possession of the material we required. Manning willingly accepted the vouchers I tendered when he found his little bluff would not work.

I have been particular in describing this incident, as Colonel Walker, in his account of it, has implied that I trampled the flag under foot by his order.

As I happen to take an equal pride in my English birth and American citizenship, and would dislike to be thought capable of disgracing either, it would have required greater provocation than the ill temper of a vulgar individual to cause me to offer an indignity to the flag of my native land.

CHAPTER X.

Departure of the second expedition—Narrow escape of Colonel Ramirez—Land at San Juan—March out to meet the enemy—Battle of Virgin Bay—Visions of empire—I obtain a furlough.

ON the 23d of August we sailed again from the port of Realejo for the Meridional department. As we were floating out on the tide, the schooner San Jose was anchoring in the harbor. She had probably been in at San Juan on her upward voyage from Costa Rica, therefore Colonels Walker, Valle, and I went aboard of her, hoping to gain information that might be useful to our projected landing there.

As we neared the San Jose a small boat put off from her side. As she passed us at no great distance, we strove to identify the muffled figure in the stern, who seemed equally desirous of avoiding recognition.

Mendez, just then hailing us from the deck of the schooner we were approaching, our attention was diverted, and the traitor Ramirez, thus favored by luck, escaped vengeance from our hands.

Mendez, though but just returning from his enforced exile, did not hesitate a moment in deciding to return with us. It was his destiny, he said, never to miss a chance of getting knocked on the head. He said that Ramirez had excused himself for deserting us before the enemy at Rivas, by pleading the orders of his commanding officer, General Muñoz.

Baffling winds blew us about the ocean for six days. The Asiatic cholera broke out on the ketch among our native troops, those on the Vesta being fortunately exempt from the dreadful scourge, though one or two of the Americans had died of it in Realejo.

We landed at San Juan without opposition.

General Santos Guardiola was in command of the enemy at Rivas. He had suffered defeat at Sauncé from the troops under command of General Muñoz, who, however, lost his life in obtaining his victory.

Guardiola had a reputation for cruelty similar to that of Mendez, being surnamed the "Butcher," as he usually slaughtered his prisoners.

So far from his name causing dread among the little force of Democrats who had isolated themselves from their friends in this far-away spot, the undoubted alternative of death only nerved them for victory. Walker no longer showed his former impatience. Ever ready to meet the enemy, he no longer disdained to seek the advantage, or at least an equality of position. While we were in San Juan, the steamer from San Francisco arrived, and the passengers from the Atlantic side of the transit route. The enemy had not yet appeared, but we had reliable information of their preparations to meet us. To show that we did not intend to disappoint them, the Vesta was sent away, and we marched slowly over the transit road towards Virgin Bay, in which vicinity they were supposed to be awaiting us.

At the half-way house we learned that they were in the neighborhood about six or eight hundred strong, under the noted Guardiola. We bivouacked for the night in some fallen timber on a hill-side. They did not make their appearance by daylight, so we resumed our march to Virgin Bay.

I ordered breakfast at the hotels for the Americans, General Valle taking charge of the guard and outpost duty with our native troops.

Modern philosophy traces about all of the

progress of mankind in civilization and the useful arts to that awakening of the intellect produced by the necessities of our nature. War is perhaps the most prolific creator of such necessities.

It is fortunate if a useful moral can be deduced through a process so hideous as that of human slaughter. The mere detail of battles seems to me revolting to the finer instincts of our nature. The Americans stacked their rifles under a guard, in front of the hotel, where they were getting breakfast. We had received notice of the near approach of the enemy. I was leaning over the rail of the porch of the Transit Company's store-house, conversing with the agent, Mr. Cortlandt Cushing, whom I had persuaded so to arrange the various packages of trunks and merchandise within the building as to afford a partial protection to those citizens, women, and children, who would instinctively seek the protection of a powerful neutral like that of the company agent, as soon as the battle should begin.

While thus engaged, my position commanding a vista of a quarter of a mile along the transit road, I perceived at the further extremity of the view a single white puff of smoke, followed by the report of a musket. It was that of our native vidette, firing on the advancing enemy. Tossing the heavy haversack I wore over my shoulder to Mr. Cushing, and grasping my rifle, which I never dispensed with, I took my place beside Colonel Walker at the head of the little column of Americans, who, at the first tap of the drum calling them to arms, had filed into position with the regularity of a dress parade.

Our native troops had formed with equal celerity and order, so that when the flaunting pennons and white ribbons of the enemy coming along the road at a charge were fully displayed within the village street, we were ready and anxious to meet them.

No particular strategy of movement was necessary or possible.. They came along the road at a swinging trot, their muskets at a trail. A hundred and fifty yards to their left, and in a parallel line, another body was emerging from the woods, a little farther off.

Leaving these latter to our native troops, we advanced straight upon those coming along the road.

They came on gallantly, changing their arms to the position of a charge, and then, as we came within pistol-shot of them, we made a slight oblique and halting movement, delivering our fire with coolness and precision on their front ranks.

They went down like grass before a scythe, their bodies and the severity of the fire abruptly checking their advance.

Then they delivered their fire at us, Walker going down at the first volley.

As I was beside him, I assisted him to his feet, when he quickly assured his alarmed men that he was not seriously hurt.

A bullet had grazed and scorched his throat, while another had passed through a packet of letters in his coat-pocket.

Their fire, fortunately for us, was rather wild and ill-directed, but sufficiently close to give us many narrow escapes.

Every rifleman, as he hastily rammed his cartridge down and brought his rifle to his shoulder, made a sure shot, and they were unable long to withstand the severe punishment they were receiving.

As they gradually edged away to some broken ground in the vicinity, closely followed by the Americans, we had leisure to note the progress of the fray between Colonels Valle and

Mendez with their troops opposed to a much larger body of the enemy who had deployed in their front from the contiguous woods.

Our natives, though fighting stubbornly, were making no headway against their numerous assailants, who were, in fact, gaining ground on them. Walker directed Captain Hornsby to take some of the riflemen and go to the aid of our allies.

Only a few followed Hornsby, I among them. As we came on the theatre of action, the most conspicuous figure in the enemy's front was an officer on a white horse, who was gallantly urging his men to charge.

The first result of our advent was the pitching of man and horse promiscuously to the ground. We afterward ascertained that the officer was Colonel Arguello, the same who had reinforced Colonel Bosque in our previous fight at Rivas.

I was felicitating myself on the check we had given them, when an exceedingly sharp, stinging sensation in my side warned me that I was hit. So great was the pain, that I sank to the ground, remarking to Doctor Jones, who was behind me, as I handed him my rifle, that I had got it this time, I thought, "plumb through me."

Jones' reply was the exclamation "Look out!" running at the same time with the rest for the corner of the nearest house. The enemy were making a determined charge, and actually passed over the ground on which, for some seconds, I lay, unable to rise. When I at last succeeded in staggering to my feet, their white uniforms intervened between me and the houses from behind which our men were firing.

Doctor Jones, whom I lately met in San Francisco, when I gently reproached him for abandoning me, replied that, for a man shot "plumb through," as I had described my situation to him, I did some of the most creditable running through the enemy's ranks to rejoin my friends that was ever witnessed. The bullet had struck the broad buckle of my sword-belt with such violence as to produce a contusion of great severity, from which I suffered much afterwards.

After Colonel Walker, with the Americans, had succeeded in driving that portion of the enemy opposed to them completely off the ground, they came to our assistance with the rush of a whirlwind. Thus reinforced, we made a general advance, and soon cleared the town of all the enemy who could get away.

The victory was complete, and so demoralized were the enemy that, taking advantage of the shelter of the contiguous woods, they disbanded to their homes, leaving Guardiola to re-enter Rivas with a mere squad of the eight hundred picked men with which he had sallied forth with the declared purpose of driving the heretic Americans into the sea.

We buried sixty of the enemy in a trench by the side of the transit road, as many more being found dead in the adjacent woods.

A remarkable result on our side was that, though many of the Americans were severely wounded, none were killed. Our native troops did not escape so well, the enemy having proved more stubborn in their attack on them.

Amidst the mutual congratulations between the natives and Americans over our victory, word was brought that Mendez was despatching the wounded of the enemy who still lay on the field. Hastening, by Walker's order, to arrest this outrage, I found the old barbarian knocking them on the head with the butt of a musket, occasionally alternating the amusement by a thrust with the bayonet.

He followed me very meekly, and after receiving the severe reprimand which Walker, in good humor with his victory and in consideration of the good services which Mendez had performed in the battle, contented himself with administering, he remarked that the Americans were not accustomed to the usages of the country; his feelings receiving a still greater shock as he witnessed the wounded of the enemy placed side by side with our own and receiving the same care and consideration.

Had Walker, indeed, sought to make this important victory a basis for the healing of the wounds engendered by internecine strife, how beneficent might have been his intervention, aided by the fusion of Anglo-Saxon energy and enlightenment with the semi-barbaric civilization of this mongrel Latin people. A people more sinned against than sinning, for they are a kindly race, by no means lacking in intelligence, but overshadowed in their liberties alike by Church and state. It will, however, be seen in the sequel it was no part of Colonel Walker's policy to foster any measures looking to a peace.

We returned the next day to San Juan and there established head-quarters for *La Democracia* of the Meridional.

Native reinforcements arrived from Leon and

every steamer from San Francisco added whole companies to the Americans. The operations in this department were under the supreme control of Colonel Walker, and he might be said already to hold the balance of power in the country, for the subjugation of the enemy at Granada was already a foregone conclusion.

I was at this time the recipient of much confidence from the man whose "strange, eventful history" came near marking an epoch in American history.

Whether the confidence implies honor, or the reverse, will be interpreted accordingly as men view political convulsions, which are rarely all wrong on one side and all right on the other, the usual partisan manner of describing them.

We took long walks on the beach, the rhythmic wave-beats seeming to emphasize the gigantic plans of empire he unfolded.

In his plan, the present popular movement was to obtain a temporary success in order to demonstrate to the hierarchical oligarchy their necessity for his aid, by which he would in the end wield the temporal power over Central America and Mexico in unison with the policy and influence of the mother Church. Then faction and Church combined would conquer a unity of power over the Central American States, with himself, of course, as the central figure.

Once united, the old boundary question—were any necessary—would furnish pretexts for adding Mexico to the Central American Empire. The United States, under the domination of Southern ideas, which were supposed to be favorable to the measure, could be relied on to vindicate the "Monroe doctrine" in saying "hands off" to any possible European interference with his scheme.

For the rest the plan was simple. Conquest was the end, and by the simple method which is epitomized in the saying, "Nothing succeeds like success." This was to be the talisman to draw to his standard not only the bold spirits ever ready to follow a leader without asking questions, but also the more timid who courted safety by an adhesion to power in any shape.

The impediments of constitutional law were, of course, considered as mere cobwebs to be brushed aside by the power which, like Louis the Fourteenth, could declare, "I am the State."

Such was the policy outlined by this bold and capable, but not sagacious man; not sagacious, inasmuch as he took no account of a factor in modern politics all powerful now, however insignificant it may have been anterior to the first French Revolution,—that of popular ideas.

As his scheme included the re-establishment of slavery in a population the majority of whom were of mixed African blood, and an affiliation of power with the Church in a time when freedom of thought had made progress, it came at too late a day in the world's history.

I listened to this conspiracy against the popular liberty, for which I had entertained a romantic attachment, and my heart was sad. He was ambitious of power, while I was merely philosophic.

" T is in ourselves that we are thus, or thus."

I was young, which is my excuse for venturing to remonstrate against the course that such a man had determined upon. As well have bid Niagara to stay its torrents. He was offended —he could now afford to be, for there were plenty of able men willing to do his bidding. I tendered my resignation, well knowing that, as victory was assured, I could be spared. If the flattering offers he made me of advancement, and the regrets of friends I had made in the army, could have solaced me for the destruction of my idols, I might have been satisfied. Mere power, however, had no attraction for me. I yielded so far as to accept indefinite leave of absence instead of resigning. I had shared the dark days of *La Democracia*. Victory over her old enemy was now assured, but for all that, Democracy, I well knew, would not be triumphant. I accepted a place in the small open boat of my friend, Mr. Temple, of San Juan. We sailed along the blue ocean near the Nicaraguan coast to the harbor of Punta Arenas in Costa Rica. A Peruvian brig was dropping out on the tide, and on her I took passage to Panama, by good luck escaping the tedious quarantine that awaited passengers from cholera-stricken Nicaragua.

The only pay or reward I received or asked for, in leaving, was an expression in writing from General Walker of satisfaction with my service. This was so cordial that the steamship company at Panama gave me a complimentary passage to New York. The *calenture*, against which I had been proof during most of the time of my residence in Nicaragua, seized me with violence at Panama, and never left me until after I had been some time at home.

The snow-covered landscape which greeted my eyes as they carried me ashore at New York offered a chilling contrast to the palm groves I had left behind.

CHAPTER XI.

Quiet of home life—Review of the acts of Colonel Walker—His successes and subsequent reverses—My return to Central America—British interference—Operations on the river San Juan—Blown up—Return to the United States.

SINCE the arrival of the Americans in Nicaragua, circumstances had thrown upon me an unusual amount of work, due in part to the experience which my longer residence in that country had given me of men and things connected with the war. As I had not spared myself in the execution of the business or military duties that devolved on me, and had suffered a good deal of physical prostration from the effects of wounds, I appreciated the relaxation of the peaceful life at home.

For a while during those quiet winter months, my dreams were full of surprises, night alarms, and all the accompaniments of horrid war. Sitting beside the cheerful winter fire, I read the press accounts of the wonderful progress of "the man of destiny" in Nicaragua, and waited silently for the inevitable *denouement* of the course he was taking.

"All unavoided is the doom of destiny."

Granada was easily captured. The accession to Walker's force went on steadily; the democratic administration of the government of the United States interposed little or no obstacle to the departure of armed emigrants from San Francisco and even from New York. The Church party of Nicaragua could make no adequate opposition to that of the people thus reinforced, and *La Democracia* was triumphant.

During these and subsequent proceedings, Chamorro and Castillon both died, and a new election was inevitable. Meantime a provisional government was set up, in which Walker, as commander-in-chief of the army, was virtually dictator. This it was perhaps superfluous to add, for those who have followed the narrative thus far need not be told that he would brook no authority superior to his own.

He was subsequently nominated for the presidency, " and elected," exclaim his unqualified adherents. So he was; the soldiers, native and foreign, being, *by decree*, enfranchised and entitled to vote for the occasion. The spirit of the dictator leaped forth at a bound. Slavery was *decreed*, not voted for—that would have been absurd. The Vanderbilt Transit Company charter was annulled by the same process, and the property seized for delinquent dues owing to the government, the plea of the company being that, as there had been two governments *de facto*, any payment to the one would not be recognized by the other when attaining supreme power. The valuable property and powerful influence of this important corporation was turned over to a personal friend of General Walker.

The power and authority of Great Britain in the affairs of Central America, derived under the Clayton-Bulwer treaty, was defied, as that of the United States under the same derivation was snubbed in the seizure of the property of her citizens, in the seizure of the transit company's property, and all this under the alliance and supposed backing to be had from the Southern United States.

Could arrogance go further? In Nicaragua itself, native applicants for office, whose families by long usage had acquired an almost traditional right to such, were coldly informed that only North American citizens would be given the places of trust. Many of these Northerners were gamblers or speculators, capable of sustaining the power of Walker by their money. There were honorable exceptions to this rule, and usually among those selected for places of trust, the men who had contributed their aid in battle were found reliable in other relations.

Many of these arbitrary acts were executed while Walker was President, others, while he was commander-in-chief only. It is unnecessary to discriminate, all originated with him.

The world gazed in wonder and expectancy, for these events followed each other with surprising rapidity. I watched them from my far-away home without any inclination to profit by the success of my former comrade and leader.

Suddenly the British Government, no longer hampered with the burden of their war with Russia, made a direct demand of the United States Government that enlistments within her boundaries for service against the peace of a neighboring state should cease. The anti-slavery party in the Northern States at the same time declaimed vehemently against the administration that countenanced the proceedings of a usurping slaveocracy.

Vanderbilt and the other owners of the transit franchises and property seized by Walker, sent cargoes of Minie muskets and fixed ammunition to the Central American opposition to Walker, now organizing in Costa Rica.

"The Man of Destiny" thus found himself cut off from supplies of men, as Mr. Buchanan dared not disregard the menacing attitude of the world, at home and abroad, an attitude chiefly attributable to Walker's slavery policy. Northern capitalists, for the same reason, withdrew their aid, and the people of Central America, excepting a portion of the Democratic faction of Nicaragua, forgot for the time their traditional hatreds, and united against a power that threatened even their personal liberty. The execution of General Coral, formerly commander-in-chief of the Church party of Granada, and of Don Mariano Salasar, a wealthy merchant of Leon, for undoubted conspiracy against the government, was an ill-judged stroke, for their treason was rather against the American domination than against the constitutional government which Walker's decrees were violating under the very thin veil of military necessity.

The men of note, including some of the most patriotic and prominent Democrats, gradually drifted to the republic of Costa Rica, and there, in conjunction with deputations from the other Central American states, aided in organizing the army for which each state contributed a contingent for the purpose of recovering the government of Nicaragua, as they alleged, from the usurpation of a stranger.

This combination might not have been sufficiently strong to have effected its purpose, had not the unwise and arbitrary acts of Walker in the matter of slavery, and his violent interference with questions which should have been left to the arbitration of the courts, caused Northern capitalists to withhold their financial support, and gave to Great Britain's assumption of moral championship the support of universal popular sentiment. In consequence of this sentiment, Mr. Buchanan had to disregard the wishes of his Southern friends, and to instruct the American naval and harbor officials to capture armed emigrants and refuse clearances to vessels carrying such. This course left Walker, with the two or three thousand American troops and the disaffected of the Democratic faction in Nicaragua, to contend against the combined armies of the Central American states, with the avenues for recruiting his constantly diminishing force nearly closed against him.

The crisis had arrived for me. I could read of his successes and those of my countrymen without regretting that I was not with them. When the story of hardships, reverses, the opposition of overwhelming numbers, came to be chronicled, I could only feel that my place was with them.

I proceeded to New York and took passage on the Orizaba for Greytown, or San Juan del Norte. I found on board, bound for the same destination, my old comrade, Lieutenant, now Colonel Frank Anderson, and General Robert Wheat, who had fought with distinction under General Alvarez in Mexico, and in the Lopez expedition for the capture of the island of Cuba. In the latter exploit he fared somewhat better than some of his companions, who were executed, while he was sent to Spain in irons. He was pardoned out of the dungeons of that country only to suffer wounds and hardships in Nicaragua, and subsequently death at the hands of his countrymen, as Colonel of the " Louisiana Tigers," in the War of the Rebellion.

Bob was a warm-hearted and chivalrous gentleman of Virginia. Among those living who yet remember him, none will gainsay the truth of this humble tribute to his memory. That he was brave as the bravest is also as well known.

There were others on board the steamer like myself seeking to rejoin the desperate fortunes of the Americans in Nicaragua. When we arrived at Greytown we found Colonel Lockridge, of Texas, who, although only a master of transportation for recruits in Walker's army, was, as such, the commanding officer of the company of men whom he was conducting to Nicaragua for Walker's service. Both Colonel Anderson and myself outranked Lockridge, but as his men had not yet been turned over to the Nicaragua service, he retained command of them.

We ascertained on landing that the enemy had compelled General Henningsen finally to evacuate Granada, not, however, until his gallant defence had excited the admiration of the world.

Walker's head-quarters at this time was at Rivas, but the swarm of enemies which the United Central American states had banded in arms against him had compelled him to withdraw the troops which had held possession of the various points on the transit route. The enemy now had possession of the lake and river steamers and the various points of defence on that line, so that our way between Greytown and Rivas, where we had hoped to effect a junction with Walker, was beset by the armed posts and garrisons of the enemy, who also had the steamers. In this dilemma Colonel Lockridge purchased the only available craft to be found, a small, open-decked river steamer, which had been condemned because of the rottenness of her machinery.

While this boat was repairing, the men were removed to the sand spit at the mouth of the river, known as Punta Arenas—Point of Sand.

The removal was made in consequence of the interference of the officers of Her Britannic Majesty's navy with our men, whom they sought to discourage by every means in their power. They represented that Walker was keeping up a hopeless war for personal aggrandizement, and was opposed both by a legion of enemies and by the sentiment of the better part of the world. Lockridge had recruited most of this lot from the wharves and slums of New Orleans, and when the Britons offered them free transportation back to the United States, there were many who were glad to leave us.

The point was hardly habitable in this the rainy season. It had no shelter and we had no tents, and were obliged to improvise loose shanties from some lumber stacked there. When the men were thus removed from the allurements of our persecutors, Captain Cockburn of the gunboat Cossack ranged his broadside to bear on our little camp at close distance, and coming to the point in his gig, ordered Lockridge to parade his men, as by order of Captain Erskine commanding the fleet, he wanted every British subject we had in our ranks. "This right of search on the high seas," which the English arrogated up till our civil war, when their pretensions received so severe a check, was then acquiesced in by the powerful American republic, with a meekness calculated to excite the wonder of the people of to-day.

We had no choice but to submit. The men were paraded by Lockridge, and about twenty accepted the immunity from danger and free transportion to the United States offered by Cockburn.

In justice to the Irish and English in our company, it is proper to state that most of these British subjects spoke with a Teutonic accent.

General Wheat, hoping to fasten a quarrel on Cockburn, pointed me out to him as a "British subject," for I had been born in England. The witless Briton, thinking to make a convert of me, actually offered me his protection!

I am afraid my language was very bad to him, for Wheat tried suavely to convince him that he ought to resent it in the manner customary among gentlemen. As a last inducement he offered to take my place if Cockburn had any scruples about matching his rank with that of a Nicaraguan officer; he, Wheat, claiming no rank other than that of an American gentleman, and as such the equal of any one. Captain Cockburn, continuing to disregard the invitation to a personal settlement, Wheat told him, much to the amusement of the grinning sailors who manned his boat, that he was sorry to see an English tar take refuge in his rank at the expense of his courage.

Harassed by these repeated annoyances, which tended to demoralize the men, who saw us helpless to resent such insults, we welcomed the little rickety steamer on which we at last were to embark, and lost no time in steaming away from the vicinity of our too powerful tormentors.

The banks of the San Juan are mere swamps for a considerable distance from the sea, so that, although we could make no landing, we were at least exempt from the danger of running into an ambush of the enemy. But after we had passed the mouth of the Rio San Francisco and were approaching the higher ground, we kept a sharp look-out for the enemy.

A few hours' steaming brought us to the mouth of the Serapaqui River.

Costa Rica claimed the territory along this river to the San Juan, and we saw the flag of that nation flying over the fort constructed at its mouth.

Steaming up within musket-range of this work, we were greeted, without other hail or ceremony, with a fusilade of bullets, which, whistling about us, notified us not only of the intention of the garrison, but, by the peculiar sound that Vanderbilt's cargoes of Minie rifles had reached their destination.

We landed a little below and on the bank of the San Juan opposite to that claimed by Costa Rica. Here Lockridge made his first injudicious move, in causing log-defences to be thrown up. Nothing is so demoralizing to men, who have absolutely to rely on themselves, as this seeming distrust of their ability.

Besides the fort at the mouth of the Serapaqui, the enemy had an earthwork opposite on our side the river. This, Anderson and I persuaded Lockridge to attack, and we carried it after a rather stubborn resistance, in which the enemy were supported by the guns across the river at Fort Serapaqui.

Our losses were trifling, but the force developed by the firing from the fort warned us that we should have a more serious job in capturing that place—a feat to be accomplished before we could ascend the river.

Lockridge was willing to entrust the affair to Anderson and myself. We prepared for the attempt as soon as Wheat had devised a kind of chain-shot composed of melted leaden balls connected by short chains, to be used in the small brass pieces which we had captured at Cody's point opposite.

We crossed the San Juan in our little steamer about midnight, a mile or two below the fort, which was on the further bank of the Serapaqui, and, as we had to cut our way through the thick jungle, we did not reach the small clearing of felled timber, which had recently been cut down at the mouth of the Serapaqui, until near daylight.

This clearing was intended to destroy the cover which the standing timber made for an enemy in attacking the fort. But, as the logs had not been removed, it offered good protection, provided the men kept close to them. As the Serapaqui was a narrow river, it was quite close enough for effective shooting by skilled marksmen.

Colonel Anderson and myself were old friends. He was hardly recovered from the wounds which were the cause of his absence from Nicaragua, and said he would give me a chance to win my promotion by leaving me the more active management of the attack.

We got well under cover of the logs before daylight, suffering but little from the uncertain fire directed on us in the darkness, from the fort. My plan was to open fire at daylight. Wheat had been instructed to open on them simultaneously with his small field-pieces, from the opposite side of the San Juan River.

Thus we established a kind of triangular

fight, with the advantage of occupying two of the angles ourselves.

The firing for about an hour was really very sharp, and the casualties frequent on our side, for whenever a head or arm was exposed in the act of firing, the rain of bullets was pretty sure to find it. By the slackening of their fire we judged the opportunity to have come ; we charged by fording the shallow river a little above, surprised at the time that we encountered so little opposition to our advance from an enemy who had replied so well to our fire from behind the logs.

On entering the fort the thing was explained by the large number of dead we found. This showed that Wheat's artillery and our fire combined had rendered the place untenable, and that the garrison had taken to the woods.

Our own men who had fallen were decently buried, but Lockridge conceived the novel idea of notifying the British, who had persecuted us so much in the harbor of Greytown, of our victory, by throwing the dead of the enemy into the river, whose rapid current, when the tide set outward, soon carried to the sea those spared by the alligators.

The impractibility of any successful pursuit

of the enemy through the dense woods forced us to leave them unmolested to find their way to the interior of the state, and we moved our camp into the newly captured fort.

Soon after this affair, Colonel Titus, of Kansas border warfare notoriety, arrived with a fine-looking company of men. It was proposed by Lockridge that Anderson, who was the officer senior in rank present, should command an expedition for the capture of Fort Castillo higher up the river.

This historic fort, which at an earlier day had been captured by Admiral Lord Nelson, held a commanding position with its water batteries on the river. Titus, who was blown full of pride by the cheap reputation he had acquired in burning defenceless houses on the Missouri-Kansas frontier, refused to serve under any one, but offered to capture the "blank place" with his company alone.

We had information that Castillo was weakly guarded, most of the enemy being concentrated at Fort San Carlos, still higher up the river. Titus was permitted to go— a great mistake of Lockridge, who should never have entrusted so important an undertaking to an untried man.

He found the water batteries almost without defence, the few soldiers in charge retreating to the fort on the hill, as soon as the little steamer bearing Titus' command was descried approaching. Titus, without opposition, took possession of the batteries and of a lake steamer, the Scott, that he found tied up near them, and then summoned the fort above to surrender.

They replied, requesting twenty-four hours in which to convey a message, asking permission for the surrender, of the commandant at Fort San Carlos. Titus, who had no real soldierly knowledge or qualifications, granted the request, and had the mortification, before his truce had expired, of seeing the fort reinforced by the arrival of a strong detachment from the fort above, so that he had barely time to cut his two steamers adrift and get from under their guns, leaving the passage of the river far more formidable than before.

We ascertained afterwards that when he first demanded the surrender of the fort, it contained a mere corporal's guard, left for purposes of observation. By such mismanagement in details great undertakings are often frustrated. This opportunity lost, the men began

The "Filibuster" War in Nicaragua. 187

to show signs of discontent and insubordination. The Kansas troops, though fine in appearance, wholly lacked discipline, and desertions became numerous. They actually constructed rafts during their night watches, and men and officers floated down the river to Greytown, leaving the camp unguarded. So demoralized had the condition of the men become, that Colonel Anderson, with some few others, had nearly decided that our only chance of rejoining General Walker at Rivas would be to take passage to Panama, and thence to San Juan del Sur, when the arrival of Captain Marcellus French with a company of Texas Rangers gave us hope of forcing the passage of the river. These men were of the kind equal to any thing requiring courage and skill in action.

The entire command was at once embarked on the steamers, and when we came near fort Castillo a landing was effected and a reconnaisance in force made of the place, by way of Nelson's Hill. From this point some of us managed to get within plain view of the Fort from the land side. Unfortunately a deep ravine intervened, and this was filled with abatis and various obstructions to a quick assault, which had to be made down one hill and up another, in the face of a complete park of artillery and a vigilant and numerous garrison on the hill above.

We unanimously decided that its capture without artillery was impracticable, and, as the river front was equally well guarded, we had to abandon the attempt of passing up the river with our fragile steamers. It was decided that a few of us, with the Texans, would return down the river and join Walker by way of Panama and San Juan del Sur, leaving the mass of the troops, now utterly worthless, to be managed by Lockridge as he might see fit.

We reëmbarked the Texans, and the best of the men being put aboard the Scott, the best steamer, we left the rest to make their way by the other as they could.

The enemy had lately developed an activity in inverse proportion to our own, having been frequently seen scouting near Fort Serapaqui. Therefore it was deemed prudent to make a reconnaissance before attempting to pass that point. The head of the Scott was grounded on a sand bank, and a small party landed for that purpose.

I was watching them as they wound in and out among the trees, my elbow resting on the window-sill of the pilot-house on the upper deck of the Scott, when suddenly I felt myself hurled into the air with terrific force. The engineer had pumped cold water into the superheated cylinder, and the boiler had burst, tearing the entire front of the boat into fragments.

Bruised and mangled from contact with the splinters and debris of the wreck, I yet retained consciousness and with it an unusual clearness of intellect. Perfectly aware of what had happened, I could speculate on the end which seemed at hand, and even entertain a vivid curiosity to solve the problem which had afforded me so much labor of thought in life—"that something after death."

The shock that dissipated these fancies was when, amid a thousand fragments, I struck on what proved to be the debris about the disrupted cylinder on the lowest deck. I was plunged into the steam and scalding water, from which, half stupefied, I managed to raise myself, but was utterly unable to take a single step away from the dangerous proximity of steam and fire. Flames were springing up in all directions, and the agonizing wail from the charred and bruised victims of the catastrophe arose on the air, some begging to be shot and put out of their intense pain. In the midst of these lamentations the cry of "The powder!" was raised.

About three tons of this combustible were piled on the upper deck, its weight having caused the breakage to terminate just where it was placed. The tarpaulins which had been thrown over the powder to protect it from the sparks from the chimney were ablaze, and the sight caused a temporary panic among the unhurt men, who were instantly scampering for the woods. I could only gaze at it and wonder how soon the second and final act would come.

But the voices of Anderson and honest Bob Wheat were raised for volunteers, and leading the way, they scrambled up the wreck and tore the flaming canvas away—and yet they were called "Filibusters." They next came to my rescue, lifting me tenderly over the wreck. At my urgent request they laid me in the cool water of the river, for my sufferings from the boiling water and the steam were intolerable. The surgeon next came, and would have proceeded to dress my wounds at once, but after giving his opinion that, unless seriously injured by the steam, I should recover, I begged him to see to those whose screams denoted agony of suffering.

About twenty were killed, and many more badly injured.

The entire command had to be taken aboard the little steamer, in which we were conveyed to Greytown. The English war vessels were still there, and their officers vied with each other in rendering aid to all. Most of the men accepted free transportation to Panama.

I had been both bruised and severely scalded. A German, who was an inhabitant of Greytown, moved solely by pity for my situation, had me conveyed to his house, and although I told him I could not recompense him, he and his kind Irish wife bestowed untiring care and attention on me. The British navy surgeon constantly attended me, and brought me delicacies from the navy stores. After many weeks I was able to take passage to Panama, and thence, much enfeebled by the physical shock, I went to the United States.

CHAPTER XII.

The Americans beleaguered in Rivas—Accept terms from the enemy—They leave Nicaragua—Subsequent efforts at return—Tried for violation of the neutrality laws—Acquitted—An expedition from Mobile—Evading the revenue cutter—"Over the blue waters"—A shipwreck—Rescued—Life on a coral island—Return to Mobile—Take leave of Walker—His subsequent expedition and death.

THE failure of Colonel Lockridge to force a passage by the river San Juan, and thereby open a way to reinforce Walker, beleaguered in Rivas by an overwhelming body of the united troops of the Central American states, was the virtual cause of Walker's ultimate defeat in Nicaragua.

The allied army, it is true, failed to rout the small body of heroic men, but the result of the repeated engagements was a steady and rapid diminution of the Americans, who gained nothing by the destruction they inflicted on the enemy, whose ranks were constantly replenished by forced levies. The end was evidently only a question of time.

Captain Davis, of the U. S. sloop-of-war,

St. Mary's, then in the harbor at San Juan del Sur, seeing that, without outside aid, Walker's handful of brave men must be destroyed, for Walker would never compromise, sought and concluded terms with the enemy. It was agreed that Walker and his officers should leave Rivas, retaining their side-arms, and embarking on board the St. Mary's, while the soldiers and adherents of his government—native and foreign, were granted amnesty and the privilege of remaining in or leaving the country.

Favorable as these terms would seem for men who were reduced by hunger, disease, and death, almost to extremity, Walker always assumed that he was in a manner coerced into accepting them by Captain Davis and his own officers. And, in this assertion he was, doubtless, strictly sincere, for I think he would have preferred to fight to the last man.

He had no sooner set foot on his native soil than he began to prepare an expedition by which to retrieve his fortunes and reassert the rights which he claimed to have been unjustly dispossessed of in Nicaragua. That he and his adherents had acquired rights, vested and political, is not to be gainsaid. How far they were forfeited by armed violation of the constitutional laws of the nation, I must leave for others more competent to decide.

Questions of this nature are not habitually settled by the courts in Nicaragua, nor would such an appeal have suited the impetuous nature of the man who had in various ways already defied the public sentiment of the world.

I shall pass over the various efforts of Southern congressmen and others to induce the government of the United States to hurl defiance to the world in favor of maintaining the rights of the Americans in Nicaragua. England, no longer hampered with her Russian campaign, demanded of the United States that enlistments for service against the peace of her Nicaraguan ally should cease in this country, and the powerful anti-slavery party of the Northern States reëchoed the cry, insisting that no government aid should be given to establish slavery in Central America.

The President endeavored to steer a middle course, hoping thereby to retain the good-will alike of the South and the North.

Vessels were permitted to be fitted out and to start from ports of the United States, filled with armed emigrants, but the personal inclination of the captains of our navy regulated construction of the ambiguous orders given about detaining these vessels. The consequence was that Walker was detained and his force disbanded at Punta Arenas, by Commodore Paulding, and he was forced to give personal guaranty that he would make no further similar attempt.

The attitude of the English navy was such that it became imperative for the United States to instruct their own cruisers to anticipate, by watchfulness, British interference, which might endanger the public peace by exciting popular clamor against foreign intervention.

After I had recovered from the hurts received on the San Juan, I received orders from Walker to come to him at New Orleans.

A vessel was fitting out at Mobile for *colonizing* some locality in Central America. Her manifest exhibited various agricultural implements and seeds, but gave no account of the arms and munitions stowed beneath them.

While in New Orleans, Walker and some of his principal officers, at the instance of the British Consul, were summoned before the

Grand Jury, to undergo examination, on the charge of violating the neutrality laws of nations, by enlisting men for foreign service. The evidence against us was ample, and Judge Campbell's review of it seemed already to have consigned us to the limbo made and provided for such offence. The court-room was packed, for we were the heroes of the hour in New Orleans and Mobile. Colonel Walker arose, and while feigning to address the Judge, in reality appealed to the crowd. "I have yet to learn," he said, "that men, seeking to maintain their rights in the perpetuation of Southern institutions, of which they have been unjustly deprived by foreign and abolitionist interference, are to be restrained by a Southern jury, and willingly trust our case to their decision." The tumult that ensued impressed the jury, which instantly declared against finding a bill, and we were actually carried out of the building on the shoulders of the spectators.

I was entrusted with despatches after this to Mr. Marcy, the purport of which was to bespeak the non-interference of the U. S. Revenue and Naval Service in our projected departure from Mobile. A verbal promise was given to interfere as little as possible in view of the popular clamor in the North, and then, one evening after dark, Colonel Anderson and I embarked on board the schooner Susan, which had already received about a hundred and fifty emigrants. The ship being cast loose from her moorings, the tide silently carried us out into the bay of Mobile.

No customs official had molested us while fast to the dock, but when we had reached the open bay a shadowy vessel ran athwart our bow in the semi-obscurity of the night, hailing us as she passed by announcing herself a United States revenue cutter, commanded by Captain Morris. He had orders if we should persist in sailing with our present cargo, to sink us as soon as we were a marine league from the shore, that distance constituting in their parlance the open sea. This we agreed among ourselves was unpleasant. She carried heavy guns while we carried none, and besides not even Walker was quite prepared as yet to make war with the United States.

Captain Harry Maury, who commanded our schooner, was a thorough sailor, intimately acquainted with the varying depths of the bay of his native Mobile, and a true type of the oft-quoted chivalry of the South. He, furthermore had a rather intimate convivial acquaintance with Captain Morris of the cutter.

We therefore readily agreed that he should try his diplomatic talent, to extricate us from our unpleasant situation, for he assured us that Morris was a man to carry out his instructions.

As the cutter again came around within hailing distance, Maury hailed, asking permission to go aboard with a friend or two, for discussion of the situation. Receiving a cordial invitation to bring as many of his friends as he pleased, Colonel Anderson and I accompanied him.

The wind being very light the two vessels kept almost side by side while we were in the cabin of the cutter. Maury remarked that to men who were prospectively so near Davy Jones' locker, a glass of grog would not be unacceptable.

Morris, hospitably inclined, set forth champagne, drinking fraternally with those whom a hard duty compelled him to immolate, and, as bottle succeeded bottle, I saw that it was to become a question of endurance.

Perfect courtesy was sustained and still

further tested when Maury invited Morris to come aboard the schooner and try our wine, pledging himself that he should be returned in safety to his own vessel. Whatever Morris might have decided an hour before, he now promptly accepted the invitation, following us in his own boat.

Drinking was resumed on the schooner, and, as Morris was helped into his boat, Maury told him that he would not keep so good a fellow chasing us through the darkness of the night, but would anchor and wait for daylight, cautioning him not to run into us when our anchor went down.

The night had become exceedingly dark, and as the captain of the cutter reached his deck, Captain Maury called out, cautioning Morris not to run into us when we should bring up.

At the same time the order was given in a loud voice to "let go," and by a preconcerted arrangement the anchor chain rattling through one hawse-hole was pulled in at the other.

Morris, supposing he heard the chain carrying our anchor down, let go his own. As he brought up we shot ahead, and then came the delicate part of the business.

Maury had reckoned on the difference in draught between our vessel and the cutter—about six inches,—together with his superior knowledge of the depths in the bay, to carry us over by a short cut into the sea. He had arranged his manœuvre to coincide with our arrival at the spot on which he wished to make the test.

We therefore, headed directly across the channel, and Morris, quickly perceiving the trick we had played him, followed as soon as he could pull in his anchor. Even this delay gave us a start which in the thick darkness deprived him of the advantage of our pilotage. We afterward learned that he did not go far before he was fast on the bottom, and of course, had to wait for high tide to get off.

The first half-hour after heading across the channel was full of anxiety for us.

If we had taken the ground, that would have terminated the expedition; and if the cutter had succeeded in keeping on our track, and avoided the same danger, it would have been equally fatal for us. The blackness of the night was our best friend. Once or twice we dragged on the bottom, but in half an hour the lead indicated deeper water, and, as the sounds from the cutter had faded away in the distance, we had hopes that she might (as was the fact) have grounded. Nothing less would have been of service to us, for with her superior speed and knowledge of our general direction she must have overhauled us.

In this uncertainty we watched for daylight with anxiety, but nothing corresponding to the cutter was visible. The blue water and sky, and some inward bound vessels was all that met the view.

We sped onward with favoring gales over the summer sea, bright sunshine overhead and balmy airs gradually becoming more gentle as we entered the tropics. Day succeeded day uneventfully. Our principal diversion was in instructing the *emigrants* how to work the ship. They were mostly of the class found about the wharves of Southern cities, with here and there a Northern bank cashier who had suddenly changed his vocation. These men were a study, and presented infinite phases of character and diversities of education and profession.

Of course they knew nothing of seamanship, not even the names of the commonest ropes;

but we devised a plan to obviate this difficulty.

The different cards in a playing pack were fastened to the ropes, and whenever the order was given to " haul away on the Jack of Clubs or the Ace of Diamonds," there was no danger of a mistake being made. I have since seen this method alluded to in descriptions of similar emergencies, but have no doubt we were the originators of the plan.

It was also found convenient in securing prompt attention to an order requiring for execution a considerable number of men, to use the prefix *Judge* or *Major*.

" Judge, bear a hand to square the yards," was sure to bring a crowd to bear on the work.

By the shores of Yucatan, famed for ancient empire, past Cape San Antonio, we sailed across the Caribbean Sea, on the farther shore of which lay the port in Honduras where we had been directed to make a landing.

We had sailed with sealed orders, to be opened within two days of our port.

We had now attained this point, and the arms were passed up from the hold and distributed ; the men were equipped, and as the castle at Omoa was to be taken as soon as we landed, various combustibles and scaling ladders were improvised and stowed away for immediate use.

These preparations completed, Colonel Anderson, who was in command, paraded the men, and read such of the sealed orders as it was deemed advisable they should be made acquainted with.

These orders were remarkable in one respect,—to me at least, who of late had not been so intimate with the manner of conducting the war as some of the others, who saw nothing irregular in instructions that directed the seizure of the church plate and other valuables belonging to those inimical to the cause of the Democrats in Nicaragua.

When I expressed myself indignant at being expected to aid in carrying out a policy which would receive the condemnation of civilization generally, my friend Anderson admonished me to keep such scruples to myself, as Walker permitted no private judgment adverse to his decrees. I thanked him, and told him that as long as we had the enemy before us, I had nothing further to say. But as soon as I could honorably withdraw I should leave the service.

We were now in that part of the sea near the Honduras coast abounding in coral reefs, most of them submerged and only apparent to the eye and ear by the furious surging of the water against their hidden mass. This contact would often send the white spray far into the air with a deafening noise.

I had paced the deck many hours into the peaceful night, peaceful at least except where the water beat over the reefs. A gentle ripple from the sharp bows as the water was tossed aside, and the shimmer of the light on the wavelets, with the moon sailing serenely overhead, forms a picture not easily forgotten.

I went below, passing the mate and some of the junior officers wrangling over a game of cards at the table in the centre of the cabin, and threw myself, dressed, on my bed.

My head had hardly touched the pillow when a harsh grating and jar of the vessel, whose forward motion was at the same time stopped, advised me without the mate's exclamation "Struck, by God!" of what had happened.

The ship had run on one of the numerous coral reefs, and with such force as to break in the middle, where the sharp coral protruded through her bottom, holding her fast, a fortunate circumstance for us, as, if she had gone over the narrow reef, she would have sunk instantly in the deep sea. The sudden arrest of motion sent one of the masts overboard, and the large rent in her bottom caused her to fill with water almost instantly. I sprang from my berth to the floor, the water reaching to my waist. Securing my coat and pistol, I groped my way through the water to the deck, a difficult task, as the ship had careened and lay on her side. On deck, where I had left every thing so peaceful, how great the change! The resistance offered by the vessel to the swell of the sea, caused the water to strike her so violently as to dash the spray in clouds high over the deck.

The fallen mast held against the leeward side by the standing rigging, which remained fastened to the deck, thumped the vessel so heavily that it seemed as if it would beat her to pieces, while the remaining mast strained so hard that there was strong probability of it wrenching the hull from the reef which alone held it afloat.

The *emigrants* were indulging in wild lamentation over the apparently inevitable death that awaited all alike. Prostrate on the deck they seemed given up to despair.

I confess, as I looked abroad over the seething waters under the moon's pale beams, it seemed to me that I would have preferred a death on the battle-field, but with the mechanical instinct acquired in a life of emergencies, I struggled over the prostrate forms on the deck to that part of the side where the beating mast seemed to threaten instant destruction. Here I found Maury calling for an axe, which was soon brought, and a few well-directed blows severed the hamper, released the spar, and lessened the noise which, with the dashing water and yells of the men, was frightful.

The axe was next applied to the mast left standing, and this soon went after its fellow. Relieved of this burden the ship partly righted, and Colonel Anderson and I next turned our attention to quelling the disorder and turbulence of the men.

A gang of the most excited were trying to lower the only small boat from the davit by which it hung at the stern of the vessel, their numbers impeding the work, as they most certainly would also swamp the boat the moment she touched the water. Persuasion would have been thrown away on these maniacs, whom we dashed to right and left, and, with cocked revolvers pressing them back, succeeded in clearing a space until we were seconded by others, and enabled to station a guard over this fragile but only craft we possessed for seeking aid from some perhaps not distant land or passing ship.

This was no sooner effected than word was brought that some of the men were in the hold of the vessel, drinking themselves stupid from the contents of the spirit casks.

We found them crowding over a cask, the head of which had been knocked in, ladling the whiskey and drinking it from tin cups as if it were water.

Our authority, backed by the pistols and the prompt kicking of the casks, opened and unopened, over in the bilge water quelled the disorder, though fierce threats were indulged in, the men claiming the right to drink themselves insensible in view of impending destruction.

This, though far from feeling assured of ourselves, we persuaded them was not necessarily certain, but we began to regain hope as we saw the ship did not settle, and we were reassured, after an examination, by finding that since she was relieved of the masts and wreckage the hull remained in about the same position.

A high sea would doubtless lift us off the rocks, but at present, though the spray continued to dash furiously against the windward side of the vessel, the water was smooth a little distance away.

A calmer feeling gradually pervaded the men as they saw those of us in command preserve a hopeful view of the situation, and as the moon was nearly at the full, we had her light to cheer us through the remainder of the night. Huddled under the weather bulwarks or wherever shelter and holding-ground could be obtained on the slanting deck, we awaited the coming of daylight in dread anxiety, lest the beating surges should scatter the remaining fragments of the ship over the waste of waters.

The dawn at length broke, quickly followed by the effulgent tropic sun whose rays, darting over the broad expanse, revealed the desolation by which we were surrounded.

A glimmering ocean filled the field of vision; here and there a patch of white water indicated the hidden reef, and in one spot to leeward, amid a larger surface of foam than usual, a dim, brown patch showed that the coral rose above the water, forming a little island or sand quay, a home of the turtle and the sea-gull.

In our immediate vicinity the water foamed over ledges of coral plainly visible, the ragged pink branches seeming but a few inches below the surface of the blue water. These coral forests, whose tops came so near the surface as to cause the sea to break furiously over them, often have many fathoms of water close to them, so that the winding channels of deep sea were traceable like blue ribbons amid the pink coral.

The man who was last at the wheel, one of the ex-bank cashiers, as well as the officer of the watch, must have been singularly remiss in their duty, for the white water which extended all around us ought to have warned him of danger.

As the deck inclined at a considerable angle, owing to the ship's lying nearly on her side, it was difficult to move about. As soon as the mid-day sun permitted, our bearings were taken, making us distant about seventy miles from the British settlement of Balize, Honduras,

The coral on which we had struck was marked on the chart as Glover's reef. After a brief council, the small boat which we had rescued from the men was lowered, provisioned, provided with a sail, compass, etc., and given in charge of the mate and two men, with instructions to proceed in the direction of Balize or of any vessel that might be encountered.

We watched the departure of this frail object, our best hope of succor, with intense interest, and when the horizon shut her from our view, we turned with not less solicitude to watch the wind, speculating on the portent of every little cloud which might develop a wind that, by agitating the sea, would indubitably lift us from our hold on the coral and consign us to the sea.

As there were many spars and casks about the ship, these were collected and a raft built, to be used as a *dernier ressort* in case the ship would go to pieces, but on getting the men on it for trial, it sank two or three feet under their weight in a calm sea, demonstrating that, in rough water, it would be wholly useless.

Three days we remained on the wreck, our food consisting of raw pork and biscuit—for the galley had gone overboard with the masts. There was, however, no complaint of the fare, or the cooking ; a notable example of the evolutionist theory of adaptability to environment.

During this time one or two vessels had passed on the far horizon but none was expected to come within sight of our coral environed locality. On the fourth day, what at first was thought to be the wing of a gull, became soon apparent as a small fishing boat, at first heading for the distant white water already mentioned as bearing evidence of contiguous land ; soon, however, we had the satisfaction of seeing her course changed directly for us.

In an hour she was alongside, having threaded the devious channels between the coral with a skill that betokened a knowledge of the navigation which could only be a result of long practice.

Her occupants inhabited the small island of coral ten or twelve miles distant, and were returning from their market at Balize, whither they had conveyed a cargo of fish, green turtle, and cocoa-nuts.

They readily took as many of us on board as they could carry away at once, promising to return as often as was necessary, for our abandonment of the hulk constituted it their flotsam.

By night we were all on the island, which on a nearer approach we found to consist of about thirty acres in surface, raised a few inches above the sea and covered with pure white sand, through which—fertilized by extensive ammoniacal deposits of fish remains—there shot up a continuous grove of cocoa palms, laden with fruit, and, in consequence of the entire freedom from underbrush amidst their tall stems, forming a canopy with their broad leaves from the sun's rays, and giving every facility for walking that could be had in the most elaborately kept park.

This lovely spot was protected from rough water by outlying reefs breaking the force of the sea, and at night, when the moon's beams filtered through the palm foliage and the murmuring ripple of the sea broke in gentle cadence on the shelly beach, one might easily imagine himself transported to one of those abodes of the blest which I am afraid we lose sight of with the fairy stories of childhood,—lost perhaps in fruition, but not in idea.

Even yet I sometimes fancy the possibility of a return to that fairy island. The flickering moonbeams doubtless still shed their soft light over the tropic foliage and on the glistening sand; the sea still murmurs its sad chant so full of nature's sweet music to the appreciative, so discordant to the mere worldling. There are other feasts than those of the wassail, other pleasures than those sought by the votaries of fashion and wealth. A peaceful communion with nature and with men's highest thoughts on life's meaning, may yield greater and lasting joy.

A fish and vegetable dietarian would have been delighted with the products of this island. Conch and green-turtle soup, fish in great variety, cocoa-nuts, yams, plantains, and bread-fruit, all in great abundance, formed a pleasing change from the biscuit and raw pork of the previous days, and as our ship's stores were all saved we had no reason to complain of our commissariat.

Eight days, including Christmas, we remained on this charming spot, and then the smoke and afterwards the hull of a large steamer were descried on the horizon.

Our native friends went out in their boat to

pilot her amid the coral reefs, and, after a while, she anchored near by.

The first boat that left her side was that of our ship. The mate had arrived at the British settlement for the logwood-cutting, and found in the harbor Her Britannic Majesty's sloop of war Basilisk. He no sooner mentioned our destitute and dangerous situation to her captain than steam was got up, and, without an instant's hesitation, the huge vessel came to our relief.

A few questions put by the captain to the mate acquainted him with the nature of our enterprise, which was opposed on general grounds by the British nation. But they chose to view us as shipwrecked people only, and, with the humanity characteristic of the nation generally, and of the British sailor specially, came without question to our aid.

We were all taken on board the beautiful and magnificent ship, and her captain, desiring to make the favor complete, declared he would land us at our home if we so desired. Five days over the blue water the majestic vessel, propelled by wind and steam, held her way and landed us free of charge, together with our valuable stock of commissariat stores saved from the wreck, on the quay at Mobile. As we steamed up the harbor, we passed close by the anchored revenue cutter, whose pursuit we had evaded on the outward passage. A spontaneous cheer of derision was given by the returning emigrants.

Captain Maury, in relating the episode of our evasion of the cutter, to the British captain, remarked that our disaster was ascribable to sailing in a ship bearing the name of a woman (emblem of inconstancy and fickleness) and not to the cutter.

The citizens of Mobile were great admirers of General Walker, who represented in his Central American policy Southern ideas and interests. As a mark of their esteem, and of their admiration of the humane and generous act of the officers of the Basilisk, they and some of the Nicaraguan officers were given a grand banquet and the freedom of the city.

We found ourselves the heroes of the hour.

I soon afterwards took leave of General Walker, declining his invitation to take part in another expedition which he purposed leading in person, frankly telling him that I believed the methods he was adopting for compelling a recognition of the rights we had won in Nicaragua were not likely to prevail against the declared hostility of the world.

His reply was charateristic:

"I am not contending for the world's approval, but for the empire of Central America."

The Nemesis which ever accompanies the acts of men was ready with her award. He landed with his next expedition of about two hundred men at Truxillo, in Honduras. Following his usual custom of making the alternative in his encounter with the enemy one of victory or death, he dismissed his ship before counting the strength of his foe. They had been apprised of his coming, and had assembled in numbers sufficient to overwhelm his little band, who, unlike the original fifty-six at Rivas, were cowed in spirit by the numbers opposing them.

In vain he sought to infuse his own indomitable will into his followers; they felt they were overmatched, and fought rather on the defensive than with the impetuosity which alone might have enabled them to clear a road for themselves through Honduras to Nicaragua.

Unable to break through the cordon of his

enemies, he sought to march by way of the coast to some point less beset by foes. They met him, however, at every point, and I can imagine the longing he must have felt for the band with which he attacked the barricades at Rivas. His men absolutely refused the tremendously unequal combat. In this dilemma, after several unsuccessful engagements, which demonstrated the hopelessness of his situation, he was prevailed on by the captain of an English ship, which happened to be in the port, to surrender himself to him as a representative of the violated English protectorate over the Ruatan Islands and British Honduras—to become a state prisoner subject to the jurisdiction of the English courts. The captain—whether repenting himself of the responsibility he had assumed, or actuated by baser motives, I know not—no sooner received a formal demand for his delivery by the Honduras military authorities on shore, than he basely handed him over to their keeping.

The result was easily foreseen by the unfortunate prisoner, who scarcely deigned a defence before a court where he was already prejudged. The sentence of the drum-head court-martial before which he was tried directed that he should be shot. It was carried into effect at once.

General Walker met his death with the calm courage which had been an eminent characteristic of every act of his life. He was bravest among brave men, and his freedom from vulgar, commonplace vices exalted him in life in the estimation of his adherents and friends.

In death his memory is cherished by them for the example he gave to the world of courage and high purpose.

> " He was a brick, and brave as a bear.
> As brave as Nevada's grizzlies are.
>
> . . . .
>
> A dash of sadness in his air,
> Born maybe of his over-care.
> Speak ill who will of him ; he died
> In all disgrace :
> I simply say he was my friend
> When strong of hand and fair of fame ;
> Dead and disgraced, I stand the same
> To him, and so shall to the end."

APPENDIX.

THE subject of an interoceanic way for ships across this continent, the configuration and position of which interposes a barrier to commerce between the principal marts of Europe and Asia, has in this day of increased wealth and competition attracted the attention of capitalists, of speculators, of patriots, of engineers, but most strangely its political importance and significance has failed to reach the understandings of the statesmen of the Congress of the United States. I might aptly reflect that it may be considered presumptuous in me to suppose that any advocacy of such a measure, in a work like this, should prevail, where the able arguments of engineers and officers who have devoted a lifetime in the naval service of the country have been disregarded. But *Nil desperandum*, who knows but that reiteration of an obvious fact may excite the minds of men to ponder on a question of national import in which there is neither party question nor sectional profit. Faith is said to move mountains of granite, why may it not become a solvent of stupidity?

Various schemes have been projected by private enterprise for the accomplishment of a measure conceded to be of vast importance commercially and politically. Hitherto, however, two elements necessary to success have been wanting in the different projects, namely:

capital, and that protection for capital which the ægis and sympathy of a stable government alone could give.

The various Isthmian governments, each desirous of securing for their separate localities a work that would redound so immensely to their benefit, have repeatedly granted concessions and privileges to individuals and corporations—citizens of wealthy and powerful nations—under whose protection and guaranty such a work could be successfully and safely accomplished. But hitherto—at least until the recent effort of M. de Lesseps at the Isthmus of Darien—the exigencies of commerce, combined with the implied though unwritten code of American sentiment commonly known as the Monroe doctrine, have not been sufficient, or have served to restrain the enterprise of foreign capitalists and governments, and the wonderful supineness of the American Congress on a question of such vast national as well as commercial importance has served to deter the otherwise willing capitalists of the United States from the undertaking.

That M. de Lesseps, eminent in his profession, successful in overcoming the natural obstacles in a similar undertaking amid the desert sands of Suez, and backed by a syndicate of monied men who relied on his judgment, should, though elated with his earlier achievement and the adulation which ever follows success, have imagined he could equally overcome the greater obstacles of the mountains, the treacherous quicksands, the overflow from a vast water-shed, and the pressure of the tides of two mighty oceans, only evinces that man's power in directing the forces of nature is not illimitable, and that he never extinguishes them.

Those, however, who are disposed to think that the Isthmus of Darien was his free and natural choice have but ill informed themselves of the ulterior motives which decided him to select that which is now proved impracticable, in preference to the route proposed by way of the San Juan River and Lake Nicaragua, a natural water-way of which a distinguished and honored officer of the U. S. Navy, Rear-Admiral Daniel Ammen, writes : " The exceptional advantages which exist for the construction of the Nicaragua Canal will, beyond question, bring about its construction, whether by our citizens or those of some foreign power."

But had the Paris Congress, at which it was decided to attempt the construction of a canal over the Isthmus of Darien, approved of the route via Nicaragua, they would have had to share the profit and control and glory of the enterprise with Americans whose prior claims and concessions from the Nicaraguan Government would have had to be recognized, as would also the right of interference in their behalf of the Government of the United States.

The Isthmus of Panama, on the other hand, has ever been considered a kind of property of the world,—too remote for the opèration of the Monroe doctrine, and safe, on that account, to become ultimately the possession of the French nation whenever the vested interests of her citizens shall demand, as they doubtless will, the protection of their government against the rapacity and revolutionary proclivities of the *Nuevo Grenadinos.* Who can doubt, in view of this alternative, what would be the choice of a Frenchman ; and, after all, it may suit them to become the possessors of the Isthmus, even without the canal, at the expense of the millions they will devote on the implacable shrine of nature.

The impracticability of this scheme will, however, only

stimulate the ever-increasing demand of commerce for the more feasible one by way of Nicaragua, by which the natural obstacles which have rendered the other impossible may be avoided, and the desirability, importance, and profit of an enterprise of this nature being conceded, as it has been by the effort made at Panama, and by the significant fact that capital, which is proverbially timorous, is, nevertheless, ready in abundance for a new effort as soon as such action is taken by the United States Congress as is befitting the attitude of the dominant nation of this continent in its public affairs, and as assurance to her citizens that their property invested in a measure beneficent alike to this country and to the world, would receive protection from the instability and revolutionary tendencies of the Central American governments and encroachments of foreign nations.

That the "exceptional advantages" alluded to by Admiral Ammen do exist, it is only necessary, in proof, to point to the able and exhaustive reports of Chief-Engineer Menocal, and to the invariably favorable testimony of professional engineers who have examined the route.

For myself, who, without such professional knowledge, have, nevertheless, had exceptional opportunities for observation and comparison of the routes by way of Panama and of the San Juan River and Lake Nicaragua, and who have neither present nor prospective interest other than that which every intelligent person has in a public improvement, I can add, as the testimony of common sense observation, that the latter is most favorable of access, by its latitude, for the marts of the world; possesses a natural water-way and inland harbor of sufficient extent and resource of water-shed to supply any depth of water and furnish shelter ample to all shipping; a salubrious climate, a surrounding country of great natural resources, including those for marine appliances, a favorable alliance with a neighboring state desirous of friendly relations, and which happens to possess a marketable commodity of no less national importance than that of the unique marine gate-way across the continent.

Is it reasonable or just to suppose that this great privilege will much longer go begging ;—and how can we expect to deny to other nations a right of acceptance of that which we do not desire for ourselves ?

The Monroe doctrine is a good one ; a dog-in-the-manger theory, however, is not.

The former has not prevented the inception of a foreign enterprise which, without benefiting the world, will probably result in a French ownership of New Grenada.

A persistence in the latter will assuredly cause the people of Nicaragua to seek an alliance for their favorite project with the covetous and domineering German empire, whose rulers are in vain seeking fruitful fields for conquest in the Old World, and who, failing in their recent efforts at purchase of the island of Cuba, would hail with delight an opportunity for possessing themselves of such a " coign of vantage " as they would gain in doing the police duty for the commerce of this hemisphere, with the aid of coast defences on two oceans. To those cognizant of their aggressive and domineering habits as a nation, the prospect of such a consummation would not be pleasing.

And why should any question of such possibility occur ? Every argument for a United States protectorate and guaranty for the enterprise is favorable to that end. Only some inherent weakness or defect in the Constitution could forbid such an obvious necessity. Such defect was once pleaded in favor of permitting the Southern States to secede from a federation no longer agreeable or in accord with their sectional interests, but it was wisely decided for the integrity and power of the nation to first suppress the dissent and afterwards remedy the cause—if any existed.

There certainly exists no present cause, constitutional, international, or politic, to prevent this government contracting by treaty with that of Nicaragua for an enterprise of mutual benefit over the land and navigable waters of the latter country. And there is every inducement, demanded alike by honor, safety, and economy, that we, and we alone, should hold the keys of a gate-way that gives ready access to our extensive Pacific coast possessions, rather than by any supineness on this important question surrender such privilege to a possibly hostile power.

It is true that stipulations may be insisted upon, making this a free gate-way, and thereby placing our marine in our own waters on an equality with the rest of the world as to privileges of access to our own ports.

Such methods are not in vogue by the owners of Gibraltar, of the Dardanelles, why should they be with us? Much sentiment is expended on the subject of a-free-to all canal; is it necesary? In time of peace, undoubtedly. But in case of war, or if it should become necessary to protect our extensive coast on two oceans, would not the possession of this means of shortening our communications by shipping between these two oceans be a military advantage of no slight value?

It may be objected that the rest of the world, or that Nicaragua would decline to acquiesce in such an exclusive arrangement for such a purpose. As for the rest of the world, it would be none of its business if Nicaragua and the United States agreed. As regards any objections which Nicaragua might make, they could be reconciled.

Thus, either as a private enterprise, protected in its rights by the ægis of this government, or as a measure of the government itself, intended to strengthen and protect its vast coast lines by affording quick means of reinforcement for its marine on either ocean, it is desirable that this country should control the marine gate-way across this continent. Could the *manes* of Washington, of Jackson, of Clay, of Grant, be invoked to give an expression on this question, can it be doubted what the answer would be? It is not that patriotism is wanting, but that in these piping times of peace and partisan competition, men's efforts are expended in abusing each other from a Pickwickian point and forecasting future elections, rather than in considering the affairs of the nation. Were any great exigency to arise, they would be as ready as of old to do their devoir gallantly.

It is this false security that we have to dread in considering a question like that herein treated,—a security that consigns to the limbo of future possibilities a measure that should receive the attention of the present.

Let this question be once fairly discussed, and the alternative presented of an American or a foreign Gibraltar to be established near our coasts, an American or a foreign police for the marine gate-way of this continent, and the result would no longer be doubtful.

C. W. D.

BY THE SAME AUTHOR.

THE NAVAL WAR OF 1812; or, the History of the United States Navy during the last War with Great Britain: to which is appended an account of the Battle of New Orleans. By THEODORE ROOSEVELT. Octavo, third edition, $2 50.

"This work combines with a greater degree of historical accuracy and a more careful, painstaking attention to details than has yet been bestowed upon the subject an unusual spirit of impartiality and fairness—no work so entirely able and conscientious has yet appeared relative to the maritime history of that eventful epoch."—*New Orleans Times-Democrat.*

"The first full, accurate, and unprejudiced history of the war that has ever been written . . . a history which is a marvel of justice and truth. Mr. Roosevelt's book seems destined to be the acknowledged authority upon this subject."—*Springfield Republican.*

"Mr. Roosevelt's monograph is the most accurate, as it certainly is the most cool and impartial, and in some respects the most intrepid account that has yet appeared of the naval actions of the war of 1812."—*Harper's Magazine.*

"A history unusual in that it shows very little disposition to undue national self-laudation, and none whatever to abuse or depreciate the enemy."—*London Saturday Review.*

"Mr. Roosevelt's attempt to supply an impartial work which could be accepted as an authority must therefore have been a very laborious undertaking, and he has executed it with a painstaking regard to detail and an evident sincerity of purpose which cannot fail to inspire confidence. His reasoning is close and lucid, and the figures given are copious and well chosen. His criticisms are of sterling value, and indeed by no means the least important part of the work . . . he gives stirring descriptions of these desperate fights . . . The plan of the work is excellent, while the general tone is fair and discriminating . . . it is alike valuable to students of naval history and interesting to all who take pride in the doughty deeds performed by seamen of the English stock."—*London Academy.*

G. P. PUTNAM'S SONS, New York and London.

HUNTING TRIPS OF A RANCHMAN. Sketches of Sport in the Northern Cattle Plains, together with Personal Experiences of Life on a Cattle Ranch By Theodore Roosevelt, author of "The Naval War of 1812." Popular edition. With thirty-five illustrations engraved on wood, from designs made for this work, by Frost, Gifford, Beard, and Sandham. Octavo, cloth . . $3 50

"* * * He must be a hopeless reader who does not rise from this book with a new and vivid sense of the 'fascination of the vastness, loneliness, and monotony of the prairies,' and of 'the sad and everlasting unrest of the wilderness' of the Big Horn Mountains, in addition to pleasant familiarity with their flora and fauna. * * * As already said, the charm about this ranchman as author is that he is every inch a gentleman-sportsman. Again, he is a careful observer of the characters and individualities of animals, and he is a pleasant and graphic describer of them. * * * We believe the author may safely reckon on a wide and permanent popularity with English readers, even those of them who, like the writer, have long laid aside rod and gun, and learned Wordsworth's grand lesson."—*London Spectator.*

"One of those distinctively American books which ought to be welcomed as contributing distinctly to raise the literary prestige of the country all over the world. * * * Many of Mr. Roosevelt's narratives are enriched by bits of realism which linger in the memory like snatches of poetry."—*N. Y. Tribune.*

"Mr. Roosevelt has given a peculiar charm to his book from his intense love of nature and his capacity to communicate to others his own impressions. A great debt is due him for having preserved in such a charming manner one of the most important chapters in the long history of the conquest of the American Wilderness."—*Atlantic Monthly.*

"One of the rare books which sportsmen will be glad to add to their libraries. Nothing so good of the sort has appeared for years. * * * What we like about the author is the certainty that he is thoroughly trustworthy, and we feel that we may receive his sporting experiences for gospel."—*Saturday Review.*

"Mr. Roosevelt's volume is as readable as it is handsome. * * * The author is an eager sportsman and a good writer. His pen is as eloquent as his rifle is effective. * * *"—*London Athenæum.*

G. P. PUTNAM'S SONS,

NEW YORK : LONDON :
27 AND 29 WEST 23D STREET. 27 KING WILLIAM STREET, STRAND.

www.ingramcontent.com/pod-product-compliance
Lightning Source LLC
Chambersburg PA
CBHW022008220426
43663CB00007B/1013